Q405
75E

THE ADMINISTRATOR
AND
EDUCATIONAL FACILITIES

*A book designed to encourage administrators,
architects, teachers, board members, and
others who are involved in planning, building,
and caring for good school facilities.*

JACK DAVIS
President
Western Nevada
 Community College
Carson City, Nevada

E.E. LOVELESS
Professor
Educational Administration
 and Higher Education
University of Nevada
Reno, Nevada

UNIVERSITY
PRESS OF
AMERICA

LANHAM • NEW YORK • LONDON

Library of Congress Cataloging in Publication Data

Davis, James Clark.
   The administrator and educational facilities.

      1. School facilities–Planning. 2. School buildings–
Planning. I. Loveless, Edward E., joint author. II. Title.
LB3221.D28   371.6'2   80–1445
ISBN 0–8191–1391–3
ISBN 0–8191–1392–1 (pbk.)

FOREWORD

There are many who believe that the years
following World War II will be remembered as the
"golden years" for school plant planning, construction, and utilization. An impressive literature on educational facilities emerged during the
two decades of 1950-59 and 1960-69. New designs
related to fresh ideas on functions and care en-
riched the profession that utilized them and the
communities that built them. Facilities constructed prior to 1945 became functionally obsolete even though structurally sound.

It was no accident that the significant growth
of the literature on educational facilities paral-
leled the feverish construction of new plants recorded during the 1950s and 60s. Then came the
sudden turnaround which saw enrollments decline
rather than increase. Fewer students with each
passing year characterized public education during
the 1970s. This resulted in new facilities construction being severely curtailed. It was only
in the unusual situation where there were population shifts within a district, suburban growth
and other factors, that generated the need even
for limited new construction for education during
the last decade. The empty schoolhouse received
more publicity than the overcrowded one. Strategies to be pursued in the closing of facilities
(some of which happened to be in the wrong place
at the wrong time) became hot topics.

Very little fresh writings on educational
facilities were in evidence during the 1970s. Yet
new ideas on school plants are needed, particularly
for school administrators and school boards, whether
new construction is pursued on a large or small

scale. This is one reason for welcoming this work by Davis and Loveless. The writers are well qualified to provide yet another new and fresh look at educational facilities. Both are Stanford University graduates and were well schooled in this area of specialization. Both are now in Nevada and have enjoyed varied experiences in educational facilities planning and utilization. They approached this writing assignment with impeccable qualifications.

What is produced by the team of Davis and Loveless is a comprehensive, authoritative, yet concise volume. It examines educational facilities from conceptualization and planning to utilization and understanding of how facilities can best function. The writing style is precise. The logical organization enabled Jack Davis and Ed Loveless to review all the important dimensions of school plants in a minimum number of pages. The professional in the education field and the student in the classroom will both appreciate that, along with the easy reading style.

A review of the chapter headings provides the early clues to the broad sweep of the subject matter covered. Witness, "Administrator Roles" in planning, the practical consequences of "Educational Specifications," the functions or contributions of facilities as "Learning Tools," the importance of "Utilization and Care," the challenges of safety and "School Vandalism," etc. In short, the major ideas are here as are their practical consequences. In short, Davis and Loveless did not sacrifice important subject matter for the sake of brevity.

This volume should prove to be a welcome addition to a professional's bookshelf of relevant and up-to-date writings on significant dimensions of education. It is a timely piece as well, for as enrollments move up as they are predicting to do in the 1980s, as existing facilities age, and as new learning techniques of educational functions appear, there will be increasing interest in educational facilities.

Stephen J. Knezevich, Ph.D.
University of Southern
    California
Los Angeles, California

September, 1980

PREFACE

There are many factors to be considered in the development of a complete educational facility. Facilities are conceptualized in someone's mind. A need is felt, then verbalized. Educational programs, numbers of students to be accommodated, community aspirations, financial capabilities, and fitness of existing facilities are examples of the many factors which must be taken into account.

The economy of the early 1980's dictates that planning for facilities be very carefully developed and executed. This is true whether a totally new facility is envisioned, an addition to an existing facility is contemplated, or the remodeling of an existing facility is being considered.

Each community and school situation is unique. Yet there are many elements in planning a new facility which are common to every setting. The purpose of this book is to provide a planning guide for practicing administrators and teachers, school board members, and citizens. Careful planning will result in a facility which can serve the community for many years to come regardless of the direction future educational programs may go. This book is well designed to serve that purpose.

Paul W. Nesper
Ball State University
Muncie, Indiana

May 29, 1980

TABLE OF CONTENTS

CHAPTER III (continued)

CHAPTER IV

CHAPTER V

CHAPTER VI

CHAPTER VII

CHAPTER VIII

TABLES:

CHAPTER I

THE ADMINISTRATOR'S ROLE IN

FACILITIES DEVELOPMENT

The administrator is assigned many important functions as the executive officer at the attendance center levels. One of his/her high priority concerns is administering the educational opportunities within a learning center. This includes identifying possible pupils, admitting, registering and enrolling them in a variety of learning experiences, scheduling instructional activities and exercising curricular leadership. He/she also plays the role of leader of students and professional personnel at the attendance center level. The administrator is a change agent, an educational analyst, and a decision maker as well.

Of no less importance are the responsibilities an administrator has at the elementary, middle or senior high school level for the management of resources used in the attainment of educational objectives. Fiscal resources as well as facilities contribute to the realization of educational objectives. This volume focuses on one of the many leadership challenges which confront today's administrator, namely the responsibilities and contributions to the design, utilization and management of the facilities.

Without a building, a site, and the necessary instructional equipment, it would be difficult if not impossible to administer an educational program. The building level is where things happen. Without a well designed and functional structure, it would be difficult to fulfill inspiring and idealistic educational objectives. Even those who talk about schools without walls should recognize that learners must be in some kind of a site or structure which for a period of time performs educational functions.

School facilities today are more complex than ever before. Such facilities include a site, a physical structure, an arrangement of spaces, a set of special environments, and a cluster of specialized tools called furniture and equipment. When it is all put together, it is known by the name of school plant. The favored term today is educational facilities or instructional facilities, whereas twenty years ago it was the school plant and prior to that it was simply called the school building. Learning, teacher-pupil interaction, and community contacts occur here. More than simply an educational center, a school may also serve as a community center and as such can be a source of either pride or despair. It may not look like the little red schoolhouse of old. The image has changed and doubtless will continue to do so in the years ahead.

An educational facility evolves. It experiences a life cycle: planned (effectively or ineffectively), designed, constructed, cared for, remodeled, and sometimes even vandalized. The administrator has, or at least should have, an important part to play throughout the life history of the educational facilities where he or she performs the leadership and administrative responsibilities. This volume attempts to define and describe the roles, concerns, and contributions of the administrator during the complete life history of the building and its site. Much has been written about the roles of specialists in educational facilities development and management, but practically nothing has been said of the dynamic role of the administrator in this process.

This chapter focuses on the planning of a new set of facilities destined to be used by either elementary, middle, or senior high school pupils. Basically, the process of planning and most aspects of facilities management will be very similar for administrators serving at all school levels. The focus of attention may shift from one aspect to another and the complexity of the structure's equipment may vary, but the basic processes of facilities planning and design remain fairly similar. This will be emphasized in some of the practical problems being confronted by the administrator and the planning team.

In this volume, the school plant is perceived as the largest piece of instructional equipment, heavily influencing many if not all aspects of the teaching-learning process. Protection of the occupants is important, but not any more so than fulfilling educational objectives. The school plant is a means. It can grow old. Obsolescence is more likely to be of a functional rather than a structural nature. Remodeling can reduce the degree of functional obsolescence in old structures which tend to stay the same while educational demands change.

Chapters that follow will review other aspects of the administrator's responsibility for management of plant operations and maintenance of a multi-million dollar structure. A special section will be devoted to security problems and vandalism, which have emerged as matters of considerable concern to administrators. Some of the issues in new types of facilities and education will also be reviewed. First the focus is on the new as a representation of the ideal to be obtained in the development of functional facilities that fulfill their roles as facilitators rather than as inhibitors of educational processes.

PLANNING AND THE PLANNING TEAM

Functional school plants do not build them-

selves. Planning is necessary to increase the
chances of a functional plant design that facili-
tates the kinds of activities conducive to a
quality learning product. Many administrators
during their professional careers will be faced
with the responsibility of submitting recommendations to the school board or architect on the
educational design and construction of a new
school plant, an addition to existing facilities
or the remodeling of certain areas.

The administrator usually does not perform
this task alone, but as a member of a facility
planning team. On this team will be architects,
special educational consultants with expertise
in facilities planning, state department of
education personnel with responsibilities for
school plant design, school board members, the
superintendent, people in the community, and
students. At the building level will be teachers,
department chairmen, as well as custodians and
other staff members who may be involved in the
planning activities. In short, the administrator
must interact with others.

Particularly the administrator will be thrust
into a leadership role of the facility planning
team that includes personnel working at the attendance center level. The administrator must understand his/her relationships as well as the contributions and limitations of the planning team at
the attendance center and/or higher levels. He
or she must know how to work with colleagues as
well as with architectural, engineering, and construction specialists concerned with providing a
functional facility for learners.

Planning has been called intelligent cooperation with the inevitable. It is a future oriented,
complex process demanding time and resources. Often a set of specialized, if not sophisticated,
techniques is used in the process. Literature on
planning exists which can be consulted by those
interested in some of its technical aspects or

specialized techniques. Focus here is on the sequence of activities within the planning process which enables the administrator and other members of the facility planning team to express the characteristics of specialized environments of spaces desired in a new school plant, a new addition, or a remodeled area.

The planning team, headed by the administrator, is part of a larger network of planners. The services of a competent architect with interest or experience in designing educational facilities should be employed for the educational planning team at the earliest level. The architect and the staff of engineers can provide significant services early in the planning process such as: (1) on-site selection and development; (2) cost estimates for construction; and (3) essential information needed to create a viable facility design for functional utility. In addition, if the architect joins the planning team early, he will more clearly comprehend the educational philosophy, objectives, or rationale behind the proposed facility. This will help insure that the plant will indeed be a spatial interpretation of the educational program.

For similar reasons, early in the process an administrator should request involvement of a competent educational facility planning consultant. This consultant draws on his expertise and experiences to provide the planning team (headed by the administrator) with a great deal of information concerning innovative developments in facility planning and practical suggestions for converting planning concepts into space design. Larger school systems, in some cases, employ this type of specialist as a full-time member of the central office administrative staff. In short, the administrator along with the department chairmen, teachers, and other staff members, as a team of prime users of the new facility being planned, would find the services and suggestions of an architect and educational facilities consultant usable during the early stages of the planning process.

A competent educational facility planning consultant may aid the administrator in putting together a planning team. Generally the complete planning team at the building level should consist of the administrator, educational facility consultant, architect, department chairmen, and selected staff who are familiar with the program to be housed in the new construction. For instance, the administrator must determine what part of his/her school's program will be housed in the new addition to the school or the remodeled areas. If the new addition is to house the math and science departments, then members of such departments should be involved in the development of educational specifications. Likewise, if the new area is to include a driver education program, then the administrator should utilize driver education staff members as part of the planning team.

A planning team does not have to be limited to the above people. Central staff personnel, state department, or university personnel very possibly could play an effective role in both planning the program and developing the educational specifications.

The complexity of a facility planning process is evident from Figure 1, which depicts the relationships and possible interactions of various persons and groups involved in the process. The solid lines show direct and formal relationships whereas the dotted lines indicate an indirect relationship between parties involved. Thus, the architect is assigned the primary responsibilities for the design of the facility or addition or remodeling. Nonetheless, he cannot and should not assume the complete burden. A tremendous amount of planning and interaction takes place before as well as after the first sketches or preliminary drawings are developed by the architect.

In order to construct the right facility for the right program, the planning team must:

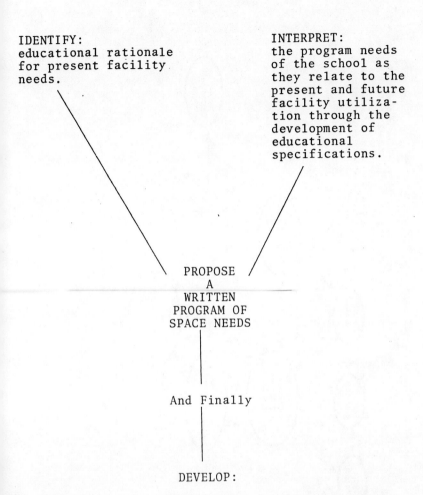

IDENTIFY:
educational rationale
for present facility
needs.

INTERPRET:
the program needs
of the school as
they relate to the
present and future
facility utiliza-
tion through the
development of
educational
specifications.

PROPOSE
A
WRITTEN
PROGRAM OF
SPACE NEEDS

And Finally

DEVELOP:

Design objectives concerning space relationships,
numbers of staff and students, special utility and
equipment requirements, special heating and acoustical requirements; traffic flow, etc., which will
provide the architect with basic detail for the
development of a design concept.

FIGURE 1. RELATIONSHIPS AMONG MEMBERS OF THE FACILITY PLANNING TEAM

lines of direct and
formal relationships

lines of indirect and
informal relationships

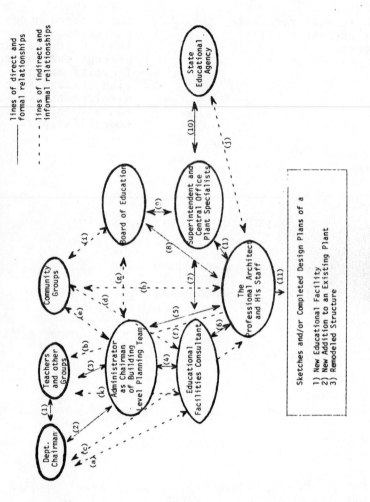

Sketches and/or Completed Design Plans of a

1) New Educational Facility
2) New Addition to an Existing Plant
3) Remodeled Structure

There are many reasons for utilizing a team approach. To begin with, school plants are complex and all trends suggest that the complexity will become greater. No one person has all the expertise needed to design a functional school plant. Every school program development is unique. No pat answer can describe a program that will meet the requirements and desires of educators throughout the land. Each new facility planning design meets the input of people who are destined to be the prime users, that is, who are going to live and work in the facility. This group is held responsible for the educational program meeting the common and the unique requirements of a given group of students in one particular school.

THE SCHOOL SITE

Many of the large school systems follow the prudent practice of purchasing sites for future school plants some five to ten years before a building is to be constructed. They may or may not employ the attendance center team, headed by the administrator, in the selection of such sites. Soaring land costs in developed areas necessitate the continuation of the policy of purchasing sites in anticipation of future building needs. This would suggest that the attendance center planning team should be involved in the site selection and should be concerned with the adequacy of the site to fulfill its functions as well as its development which may well be influenced by where the building is actually placed on the site.

A site is more than simply the locus of a building. It plays a role in the educational process as well. Outdoor physical education programs are influenced to a considerable extent by the topography, size, and development of the school site. Much the same can be said for play areas for elementary schools. Without an ample site, athletics and physical education at the secondary school level could be severely curtailed and, in addition, unnecessary parking headaches could be made for staff members, visitors, and even junior and senior high school students. Much could be said about the contribution of an adequate site to the aesthetics of the school facility. An attractive physical structure can be enhanced considerably by an appropriate and ample site that has been developed by experts.

The planning team should consult the variety of recommendations that have been made thus far on school sites. These recommendations indicate minimum standards for elementary, middle, and senior high school sites, as well as character- istics of the site such as topography, relation- ships to existing plants, and the like. At one time specific land areas were recommended for school sites. Thus five acres plus one acre for every one hundred pupils was considered a minimum for elementary school children. Ten acres plus one acre for every one hundred junior high school or middle school pupils was stated to be a mini- mum for junior high school or middle school facili- ties. Twenty acres plus one acre for one hundred pupils enrolled in senior high schools was believed to be a desirable standard at one time. Groups such as the Council of Educational Facility Planners have abandoned such fixed standards on the grounds that the minimums suggested tended to become maxi- mums and they introduced a degree of inflexibility in site acquisition and selection. Guidelines on site size can be usable if they are considered as such and not applied in an inflexible way to any and all situations.

What is done with the site is perhaps as impor- tant as its size. Full utilization from an educa- tional point of view of a given site demands care- ful planning. Usually the services of a landscape architect are required to lay out the educational areas such as physical education, driver education, camping instruction, and perhaps even outdoor en- vironmental classrooms, along with service areas such as walks, roads, parking lots, delivery

entrances, bus pick-up stations and the like.   If
the school site is to be used as a park and recreation area in the afternoons during after-school
hours, evenings, or summer months, additional design and planning problems are encountered.   Sites
for educational parks or plazas (a large educational
area serving numbers of students in varying age
groups) have received considerable attention as of
late.   This is best described as the resurgence of
an old idea applied to urban areas rather than a
new concept, and will be described in greater detail in the last chapter of this volume.   Thus, a
school administrator and his/her attendance center
planning team will also be concerned with city and
county planners.

ENVIRONMENTS FOR LEARNING

        The approach followed in this volume stresses
the creation of environments for learning rather
than brick, steel, glass, and other building materials.   Through the planning process, the concern
focuses on the kind of environment that will facilitate rather than inhibit the educational processes.
The major responsibility of the administrator and
the attendance center planning team is to define
characteristics of such environments so that the
architect can better translate them into spaces of
varying shapes, appropriate colors, satisfactory
illumination standards, and patterns.   The building
exterior envelops and encases the appropriate environment, but before this can be done the planning
team must have the capability of defining it.

        Thus the challenge facing the administrator
and his or her planning team is to define the
characteristics of the learning environment.   What
do we know about the environment and its influence
upon the program and the instructional process?
Considerable research has been undertaken over the
years to pinpoint specific characteristics of the
spatial environments.   Little research is available
to answer such important questions as the overall
effects of total environment upon the success or

failures in learning. Opinions of teachers and
educational experts support what follows as desirable, but no definitive research has done this as
yet.

One rather complete documentation of research
on various characteristics of environment is compiled in a report known as The School Environments
Research Project.1 Publications SER 0 and SER 2
(1965) identify the literature on environment projects with analyses and evaluations. These reports
indicate that lighting, acoustical, color, and
thermal factors within the schoolhouse do influence
student and teacher behavior. The Council of Educational Facility Planners support these conclusions
in its publications.2

Each of the following visual, thermal, and
acoustical environment factors deserves further
review because they are worthy of special study by
the administrator and the facility planning team.

Visual Environment

Human eyes are important sensory mechanisms
that pick up clues through observations or readings
related to human learning. The quality of the
total visual environment influences how the human
eye functions; that is, whether the eye will perform more effectively and with less fatigue. Some
experts go so far as to say that the learner sees
with his whole body. In other words, general
physical fatigue can be induced by eyestrain caused
by an inadequate visual environment.

Twenty years ago, most of the references were
to lighting (primarily its amount) rather than to
the total environment. Today, the intensity of
lighting remains important, but only as one of
several factors in the visual environment. Additional factors such as the reflectance of the
surfaces surrounding the visual task, the distribution of lighting to achieve a desirable balance
of illumination on the task to minimize glare, and

the ease of controlling the light source deserve consideration in design.

Educators, as well as architects, have profited considerably from research completed by illuminating engineers who determined the effect on learning of specific kinds of visual environments. There are a number of viewpoints in the continuing controversy about illumination standards for schools and other facilities. There is general agreement, however, that the amount of light energy striking a visual task should be considered along with such concepts as brightness difference and reflectance factors. The Council of Educational Facilities Planners pointed out that "Since 1946, the concept of brightness ratios has been considered of prime importance in the design and evaluation of lighting systems."3 Brightness difference is a term used interchangeably with brightness ratio, and deals with the variations in illumination within the total visual environment.

The specific visual task within that environment is an important reference point. A high brightness difference between the background of the task and the elements within it is desirable. To illustrate, a black letter (the element) on a white page (the background) is more easily perceived than is a gray letter on a white page. In the latter case, the brightness of the gray letter approaches that of its background. In other words, a high contrast is desirable within a visual task.

On the other hand, the visual environment should be designed to reduce the brightness ratio between the task itself and the surface that surrounds it. To illustrate, the brightness of the page of printed material being read by the student and that of the desk or table on which the book is placed should be kept as close to being the same as is possible. The white pages of a typical book register a higher brightness rating than a dark walnut desk or table surface, which results in great brightness difference.

For this reason, light desk surface materials are preferred to dark desk surfaces for visual tasks.

Visual acuity, or the ease in noting small details in a task, improves generally with an increase in the amount of light on the task and the degree of contrast between objects within the task. On the other hand, the specific visual task confronting the student should never be less bright than the surrounding area. In other words, the brightness differences should be minimized or there should be a close balance of illumination intensity between the task area and the surfaces within the rest of the space. A large body of evidence suggests that when room surfaces in which the desks and reading materials are located are significantly brighter than the task area, the quality of the visual environment decreases quite rapidly. Severe brightness differences are not uncommon in many classroom situations. Brightness is influenced by the distribution and quality of light. It is affected by the reflectance factors of the surfaces within the environment. Thus, the color of paint put on walls in a room will determine the reflectance factor. The color of the wood surface on the desk, the chalkboard on the wall, or the tile on the floor all must be considered in terms of reflectance factors. One reason for using lighter colors rather than black for the surface of chalkboards is to improve the visual environment in view of the high contrast between the black chalkboard and the surrounding wall area.

The intensity or magnitude of light falling on a surface is measured in foot-candles. Brightness, in turn, is measured in a unit known as the foot-lambert. It is related to the amount of light falling on a surface multiplied by the reflectance factor of that surface. The formula is multiplied by the reflectance factor of that surface. The formula is FL=R X FC; where FL is the number of foot-lamberts, R is the coefficient of reflection (reflectance factor) for the surface upon which the light falls, and FC is the number of foot-candles emitted from the light source. Administrators need not become experts in illumination engineering. Nonetheless, the administrator and the planning team should know enough about lighting quality standards to quiz the architect and educational consultant about what considerations are given to the quality of the visual environment.

Light within a learning center can come from natural sources, such as the sun, or man-made sources, such as the electric light fixture, or any combination of the two. Light from the sun is cheap in one sense, but expensive in another. It is very difficult to control even with such devices as building overhangs, tinted or low transmission glass, or a variety of window coverings such as shades or venetian blinds. Difficulty in distributing natural light in a room with the width exceeding twenty-two feet is great indeed unless one goes to a secondary source, such as a clerestory or plastic bubble on the roof that admits light. Man-made sources of light are more expensive because of the electricity consumed to produce light. Generally speaking, electric light sources are easier to control through arrangements of switches and the design of lighting fixtures.

Some areas of the school building demand higher amounts of light and more precise distribution patterns than others. Thus, a mechanical drawing room requires more intense and higher quality levels of illumination than an ordinary classroom. The planning team must recognize the special visual environments required for a variety of learning tasks and communicate these to the architects and engineers designing the facility.

When relating light intensity to accuracy of depth perception, there is some evidence that greater illumination results in better depth perception. However, no single intensity level appears best for all persons. There is some indication derived from tests of illumination intensity on work surfaces and muscular tension of students that muscular tension decreases as illumination levels are raised to 100 foot-candles for normal reading situations. Studies of children's health under certain illumination environments suggest improved health when visual equipment is designed to reduce glare and improve illuminating levels. Some research indicates that scores on tests in the well lighted classroom are likely to be higher than those administered in classrooms with lesser illumination levels or lighting quality.

An illumination problem encountered in most older schools and many new ones is known in popular terminology as "glare." Glare may be experienced within the room or in the area surrounding it. Large window areas allow direct glare from the sun to enter. Inside glare may be generated from electric lights, glossy ceiling surfaces, waxed floors, or highly polished furniture and equipment. Glare interferes with student perceptions and, at the same time, hastens eye fatigue. It is a qualitative factor in illumination design, occurring when there is a very high brightness difference between the task and the surrounding surfaces; that is, poor brightness balance.

Generally, enough data exists to demand that planning teams stress the design of an optimum, rather than minimal, specification for quality visual requirements. A high quality visual environment is important for schools. An optimal visual environment deserves consideration for a number of learning tasks and functions that must be performed. Individual control of lighting intensity and distribution by the teacher for different tasks is essential. Just having the control device is not enough; the administrator should assist the staff in gaining competence in the efficient use of classroom illumination.

Thermal Environment

In times past, the thermal environment was equated with heating, and was often overlooked or considered relatively unimportant in planning new facilities. In the remodeling of old facilities it was confused with the provision of heat on cold days. Of late, however, more information has been gained on what constitutes a desirable thermal environment. The total thermal environment, including the air temperature, humidity, speed of air movement, differences of temperature in the surfaces of an area, is finally receiving its just due. At one time it was believed that a desirable thermal environment cost too much. Evidence today suggests that heating and air conditioning equipment needed to produce a desirable thermal environment need not be compromised in school facilities. Much of the research being done today supports the contention that improvement of thermal environment conditions increases the productivity of workers in industry and education.

Bruce sums up the effect of facilities and thermal environment on occupants as follows: "The design and construction of buildings for human occupancy are affected by many physiological factors, the most important being the provision for a controlled and adequate rate of heat loss from the human body."4

A good thermal environment may help to attract and retain quality teachers. Evidence shows that students enjoy more and perform better in schools with a well designed thermal setting. The results of a study by the University of Iowa resulted in the following assertion:

> "Preliminary research by the Iowa Center reveals that there is significant positive relationship between the thermal environment in which children work and study and their efficiency in learning. Children did learn better under model thermal conditions. The knowledge of this relationship affords an increased control over mental functions in the

-17-

> classroom. It adds to our under-
> standing, gives us power to increase
> efficiency in learning, and places on
> us the responsibility to provide the
> favorable environment for learning."[5]

Economies gained at the expense of adequate heating,
air flow and ventilating, and conditioning of air
may well have the ultimate effect of inhibiting work
and/or learning.

A problem encountered with many of today's old
and new buildings is that little attention is given
to comfort. The heat gain problem in classrooms is
not limited to late spring, summer, or early fall
months. Heat gain may be experienced during every
month of the school year. The administrator should
be aware that sizable heat gains may result from
a number of causes such as large glass areas, high
lighting levels, mechanical devices (machinery),
and the metabolic processes of people in a confined area.

Heat gain from the sun, plus that from electric
lights and active students in a 900 square foot area
can generate up to 60,000 BTU's. On a zero degree
day, there would be enough heat in the aforementioned
area to maintain an adequate balance without the
introduction of warm air from a heating system. If
the outside temperature level moves above zero degrees, the necessity for cooling the room with outside air arises.

It is important during the winter months to
begin building up the heat levels to a comfortable
temperature in the morning hours and to maintain
them at night. However, once the building is occupied by active learners, the necessity for cooling
may supersede that for heating. Clearly, conditioning the air is a year-round problem.

In past years air conditioning was considered
by many to be a luxury. Many times it was left out
of consideration because of design problems and

-18-

costly installation, especially in older buildings. Attitudes have changed; design and cost problems have been overcome. Today, with good planning, a desirable thermal environment that includes air conditioning is within reach of most school district capital outlay budgets. This demands providing an efficient insulation product for the facility. This can reduce cooling requirements within the facility which, in turn, reduces the initial cost for air conditioning and lessens the operating cost for the entire life of the building.

A recent detailed, in-depth study of energy use for mechanical cooling by Gilles in the Orr Junior High School in Las Vegas, Nevada, clearly showed that operating costs for school air conditioning are not prohibitive. Costs for air conditioning power for classroom hours amounted to about one cent per student per day in an installation located in a hot desert climate. Multiple, self-contained modular central cooling units were serving the facility.[6]

A good thermal environmental system will allow windows to be closed and the air filtered which will, in turn, reduce noise levels and cleaning costs in the building. This can result in significant operational cost savings. For instance, for every dollar saved on maintenance in operational costs per year, many more dollars can be saved or put into additional building space.

Obviously, air conditioning is not a luxury today. It has become as important as the bricks, the blocks, and the roof. An air conditioned facility will not of itself give you a satisfactorily functioning staff, but the staff and students will function better in a good thermal environment. With a flexible, adaptable thermal environment, the ground work has been laid for a facility which will serve its occupants at an optimum level of efficiency.

Acoustical Environment

Traditionally, concerns for acoustics have focused on such specialized facilities as auditoriums, broadcasting and recording studios, theaters, churches, and elaborate office areas. However, the need for noise control in other types of construction is now being rapidly and widely recognized.

Insuring suitable acoustical separation in school buildings is now a necessity. The extensive use of glass and other hard surfaces which reflect sound; the increasing number of noise-producing machines such as typewriters, adding machines, and calculators; lower ceilings; and large class areas generate special problems in sound distribution and noise suppression. A quiet environment increases efficiency and alertness. It decreases fatigue and mental strain as well. Consequently, proper acoustical treatment of all learning centers must be a prime consideration in any school facility.

In areas where persons will be engaged in classroom activities, meetings, conferences, etc., acoustical treatment of ceilings should include some hard reflective surfaces so that voices in a normal conversational tone will be distributed throughout the area. In areas with excessive noise levels, highly absorbent materials should be used on ceilings and walls. In general, the transmission of sound from areas of high production of intense sounds such as in music rooms, shops, and gyms will disturb areas where sound areas are less intense. Zoning or isolating areas of high sound production from others is a more feasible solution than expensive sound treatments that inhibit transmission between areas. The planning team should identify areas with sound problems to the architect. The team should have the sophistication to reject poor building designs that place gyms above libraries or classrooms; music rooms next to administrative offices; or shops adjacent to general classroom areas.

Carpeting and sound control: Some school
planners have known for years that carpeting can
contribute significantly toward helping to provide
a comfortable acoustical environment for school
facilities.   The majority of today's school planners now agree that schools can profit from low
maintenance, economical, sound-absorbent flooring
in teaching spaces to help provide a better learning environment.   Carpeting has a unique capability.
Tests show that carpeting emerges as a floor covering which plays a dual role.   Carpet acts both as
a superior floor covering and as a versatile acoustical material.   Where carpeting is thought of as
a luxury item, it may be advisable to call it
acoustical floor covering.   Since carpet performs
a dual function, its cost should be compared with
the cost of other types of flooring or floor coverings plus the additional acoustical treatment required to equal that gained from carpeted floor
surfaces.   In cases where both airborne and impact
noises are a problem, carpet should be given primary
consideration as an acoustical material.   Carpets
can reduce both kinds of noise.   It not only reduces
airborne noises at the point of origin, that is, in
the source room, but it also minimizes the transmission of heavy impact generated sounds to adjacent
rooms and spaces.

Carpet offers many additional advantages for
the environment not found in other floor coverings
or acoustical materials.   The administrator must
bear these additional benefits in mind as he or
she develops a total plan of improving his/her
total school environment.   Briefly, they are:

1.   A carpet covering will muffle or
eliminate disruptive sounds of
dropping books and pencils, clicking
heels or footsteps, and scraping
furniture.

2.   Pupils can move about the classroom
more easily without disturbing others.
The scraping of desks and chairs on

the floor is eliminated, thus
reducing the tensions of irri-
tating noise. Where classloads
are becoming larger, it is imperative that sound problems be reduced
in the classroom.

3. Where the open school concept is
operational, that is, where walls
between instructional spaces are
eliminated, carpeting is most desirable to minimize learning activity
sounds from one cluster of students
interfering with other clusters of
pupils.

4. The psychological effects of carpeting
in the school facility also go a long
way toward establishing natural disciplinary controls over both the sound
output of the student and his general
behavior. Teachers and maintenance
people have noted a great reduction in
refuse being placed on the floor by
students in most carpet situations
as compared to the hard surface covering.

5. Because carpeted floors have excellent
acoustical qualities, the amount of
more expensive acoustical tile ceilings
can be reduced.

6. Carpeted floors look good and provide
a reduction in floor fatigue for teacher
and student. They provide a freedom of
motion for youngsters. Children can
sit or lie on the floor for relaxation
as children love to do. Carpet eliminates cold floors. This may be important in kindergartens as an alternative
to radiant heat in the floors.

7. Carpet can prevent injury caused by
chairs slipping from under students,

falls on stairways, and other high
accident areas.

8. Research has demonstrated that car-
    pet costs less to maintain than non-
    carpeted floors under most use condi-
    tions of traffic and soil.

Most carpet contributes an immediate sight
appeal. Because the luxury appearance of non-
carpeted floors depends on high frequencies of
cleaning, refinishing, and buffing, their maintenance costs are high in comparison to those
for carpet. For example, ordinary scuffing and
scratching which does not visibly affect carpet's
appearance must be repaired on tile, thus increasing the workload difference and maintenance cost.

Carpet's life expectance in typical, medium
traffic areas is estimated at twelve years, providing the carpet qualities are specified for heavy
use and the carpet is properly cared for. Obviously,
the life expectancy of any carpet is dependent upon
its color, type, construction, and quality. A light,
solid colored fabric not only requires added maintenance frequencies to sustain a high level appearance, but it shows fiber loss and discoloration
much quicker than a dense loop pile tweed of browns,
greys, or greens in muted tones. Certain types of
carpet are made so that individual sections can
easily be removed and replaced with little sign of
patching. These are designed for situations in
which pivot points are anticipated, such as door-
ways, corners of hallways, and the immediate access
areas to outside space.

These statements about carpet do not imply
that it is the answer to all floor problems. Certainly when floors are subjected to heavy spillage,
staining, or unusual friction, a harder, non-porous
material is more suitable. For most floor covering
situations, however, carpet will enhance the classroom environment for students and teachers.

Aesthetic Environment

Beauty has a positive effect on all. Attractiveness can be designed into a facility. It demands the concern of a planning team, for beauty does not come naturally in design. Color may enhance or detract from the aesthetic appeal of a facility.

A number of studies have addressed the problem of color selection to produce a pleasing aesthetic environment for interior spaces of the school. Evidence is not conclusive that data from color studies can direct us toward making significant decisions concerning the right color combinations for all interior spaces. The architectural firm should be held responsible for the color specialist who knows how to blend the right colors in the right places.

One study by Johnson[7] indicated that several factors influence color choices for interior spaces. The following are color selection guidelines from her study:

1. Tints of red, blue, and yellow are suitable for kindergarten and primary areas. Warm tints enhance elementary classroom objectives.

2. Secondary academic classrooms and laboratories which are settings for close visual and mental tasks appear to be the most appropriately decorated in tints of blue, blue-green, green, gray, or beige.

3. Corridors should provide visual and psychological relief from classroom decoration.

4. In general, guidance suites will be enhanced by warm tints.

5. Peach, pink, or turquoise is most

desirable for serving spaces in
dining areas.

6. Cool and neutral colors for gym-
nasiums or playrooms will offer
less distraction.

7. Green, aqua, or peach tints will
help provide a desirable setting
for activities common to the
auditorium.

8. In health service areas, green or
neutral shades are most acceptable
for physical examination areas
while yellow or pink provide a
psychological lift for sick bed
areas.

Other implications of this particular study
were that:

1. The prime factor in color choice
should be the provision of an
appropriate learning environment
to enhance the mental, physical,
and emotional well-being of the
occupants, mainly the students.

2. The selection of colors for the
school facility should be individualized to suit the particular school
under consideration, taking into
account all of its unique features.

Careful consideration must be given to providing an overall color design that will enhance the
total environment for the student and teacher.

EDUCATIONAL SPECIFICATION:
THE SPATIAL INTERPRETATION
OF THE EDUCATIONAL PROGRAM

One writer[8] began his description of the

importance of educational specifications by re-
ferring to an old Greek legend about a notorious
culprit known as Procrustes. Procrustes, according to the legend, forced his victims to conform
to an iron bed. People too tall had limbs sawed
off to insure a perfect fit. Those too short
would be stretched.

The "Procrustean bed" concept grew out of
this legend. It implies an inflexible approach
with programs or ideas stretched or cut to fit an
arbitrary pattern. It infers that preconceived
ideas will arbitrarily impose conformity no matter
what evidence there is to the contrary.

The point being made was that preconceived
notions of a school board or an architect on form
and style in architecture may produce an attractive but inflexible structure from an educational
point of view. The architect sets out to design
a building in the classical or perhaps the modern
tradition, but neglects the program implication.
A minimum of people are involved in the Procrustean
approach. The design is set and the architect pre-
pares it.

Accordingly, this writer declared:

> "The interior is divided into
> cubicles of various shapes and
> dimensions which will satisfacto-
> rily fit into the exterior design.
> A prayer is then muttered in the
> hope that the spaces thus allo-
> cated might prove useful in the
> teaching-learning process. If the
> classrooms derived in this manner
> do facilitate the instructional
> process, it is more a matter of
> coincidence than purpose."[9]

School buildings thus planned and constructed
may be aesthetically pleasing, but they end up
being Procrustean beds. No matter how beautiful

the mold into which any and all educational programs are poured, it is an inflexible mold. Within
the arbitrarily determined aesthetic pattern the
educational program is cut or stretched, that is,
in some ingenious way altered to fit to a certain
degree the spatial pattern dictated by the exterior
or physical envelope.

Many have stated that a good school building
makes great teaching possible because it is one of
the instruments necessary in the execution of the
educational program. It is more than merely an
aesthetically pleasing shelter house which protects
learners from the hazards of changing and severe
weather. The protective function gathers greater
significance when viewed in relation to the educational purposes of school buildings. When the
building is constructed and maintained to insure
the good health and safety of students, students
are, in turn, better able to concentrate more completely their total efforts toward learning. If,
on the contrary, children are housed where there
exists a constant fear of falling debris, uncom-
fortable drafts and resulting chill, poor lighting
and accompanying eye strain, incessant noise and
resulting distraction, a considerable amount of
energy must be dissipated in battling the hazards
of an undesirable physical environment. In this
sense, the protective aspects can be related to
the educational functions.

The functional school plant, then, is one
where facilitating the educational experiences is
the matter of prime concern. The materials used
in the construction and the design of this type of
a building reflect the purposes of the structure.
In other words, the curriculum finds its physical
expression in the construction and organization of
the school plant. Stated still another way, the
functional school plant is a spatial interpretation
in wood, steel, stone, brick, glass, and concrete
of the educational program.

A good looking building, one which is artistic

in nature or aesthetically pleasing, is not something to be shunned. Rather, a school structure must be functional as well as beautiful. This gives us insight into the difficulties confronting the school architect. The product of his creativity must be useful as well as an expression of artistry. Furthermore, it must be built to withstand whatever the elements have to hurl at it during at least the next 50-75 years. It will not lead the protected life of a great painting and be given pampered care by adults only. It must stand up under the romping and the stomping of active, often immature, young learners. Designing functional and artistic school buildings is an architectural challenge of great proportion.

If the planning of a school is to go beyond the process of arranging desired instructional spaces within a predetermined physical envelope that coincides with the artistic or unartistic talents of the school board and the architect, there must be a profound change in attitude and in approaches used. Basic to this change in the planning process is the recognition of the importance of the development of educational specifications as a prelude to architectural design. Just as blueprints and material specifications give expression to the physical construction, so too, do educational specifications give expression to the educational activities that are to take place in the building. Educational specifications are not synonymous with educational objectives or curriculum. A statement of the scope and sequence of educational experiences for the level of students to be housed is only a start toward the development of educational specifications for a building. Giving the architect a statement of the educational philosophy of the system plus a verbose volume entitled "The Curriculum of the School" written in the best pedaguese does not constitute adequate information on the educational specifications of a building. Supplying additional facts on the teaching methods helps, but doesn't solve the dilemma. The crucial matter is the translation

of educational needs into space requirements.
The curriculum and methods of teaching become
meaningful for school design when the spatial
implication of the program is clarified. At
this point they become educational specifications.

Functional school plants do not just happen;
they must be planned. The problem of planning a
functional school plant cannot be solved as simply
the problem of eliminating Procrustes. The legend
has it that Theseus, one of the early versions of
what we now call Superman, forced Procrustes into
his iron bed and then killed him. This does contain, nonetheless, the germ of an idea of how preconceived notions of style can be changed in favor
of function. As tempting as it might be, we must
omit Theseus' solution and concentrate on having
those who would emphasize style sleep in a Procrustean bed. The object is not to punish but
rather to help them develop a sensitivity to the
importance of function in a building. Here is a
chance for an administrator to show leadership.
Though board members and architects are not
licensed to teach and, therefore, unable to
actually use a Procrustean bed, they might well
profit from observing good teaching being limited
by inadequately designed, although beautiful,
facilities. As early as 1900, John Dewey stated:

> "Just as a biologist can take a bone
> or two and reconstruct a whole animal,
> so, if we put before the mind's eye
> the ordinary schoolroom with its row
> of ugly desks placed in geometric
> order, crowded together so there
> shall be as little moving room as
> possible...we can reconstruct the
> only educational activity that can
> possibly go on in such a place. It
> is all made for listening--for simply
> studying lessons out of a book is
> another kind of listening."[10]

Perhaps visitations and other means can make
this fact more obvious to boards and architects.

This is another step toward the recognition of the importance of developing educational specifications as a means of assuring functional school plants rather than Procrustean beds.

It is one thing to stipulate that educational specifications are desirable, but it is still another to prepare them. The difficulties encountered in developing educational specifications have many sources. One is translating what is taught and how it is taught in the classroom into space requirements--namely, the nature of the area, proportions, and special conditions needed to facilitate the learning process. Another problem stems from the fact that those who are given major responsibility for the planning and constructing of school plants are not as close as they might be to the learning situation. The architect, the school board, and the superintendent are rather far removed from where the learning actually takes place. The fact that these individuals may have at one time gone to school or actually taught in a few areas is not enough to attain expertise in all areas of teaching. Present day educational programs are of necessity comprehensive in scope, and no person can speak with authority in all areas.

Meaningful educational specifications can best be achieved through the active involvement of those who are to use the finished structure. This does not imply, however, that all you have to do to obtain a functional school plant is to form teacher committees along subject matter or grade level lines and hope that out of these committees good ideas for good school buildings will be born. The truth of the business is that individuals who have been only vaguely familiar with the space implications of a particular way of teaching do not suddenly become endowed with special sensitivity and great knowledge simply by being appointed to a committee on school plant planning.

The writers' experience in working with teacher groups in school plant planning has clearly indicated that this process has limitations as well as

advantages. Some teachers are at a complete loss
when trying to describe a desirable space for the
teaching of their subject. Others are able to tell
you what they do not like, but are not sure enough
to make positive suggestions. In planning, nega-
tive statements must be translated into the construc-
tive. Others confuse wants with needs, like the
basketball coach who teaches physical education and
declares that what the new secondary school building
needs is a huge gymnasium to seat 3,600 people for
inter-scholastic games. An analysis of the physical
education program as well as the inter-scholastic
program indicates that this is more in the nature
of a prejudice or a want rather than an educational
need. School buildings based purely on wants can
also be Procrustean beds. This is evident in some
structures with huge gyms or music rooms and little
else. Ways and means are then sought to have such
special areas used more frequently while at the
same time an extended school day is invented to
get more time out of the limited classrooms. Nor
can it be assumed that all teachers understand
fully the financial limitations under which the
building is to be constructed. Some appear perfectly willing to economize in other areas so long
as their maximum demands are met. Achieving a balance of instructional spaces can be a delicate
problem while dealing with teachers of the more
"glamorous" subjects.

The primary purpose of educational specifications is to serve as a concise and comprehensive
guide to the architect in developing sketches, preliminary plans, detailed layouts, working drawings,
and architectural specifications for a new facility,
a building addition, or remodeling a facility. Mac-
Connell, a renowned educational facility consultant,
stated:

> "Perhaps the weakest link between planning
> and building is interpreting the needs of
> those using the completed facilities.
> This problem of interpreting demands a
> fresh approach to school planning--a

formulation of a systematic procedure
for designing facilities for schools.
To accomplish a functional and economical school design, facts are needed
concerning the school program during
the initial planning stage. The proposed procedure is, in essence, a fact-
finding process--a cooperative task of
educators, students, and lay people to
analyze, describe, and interpret the
program so that it can become the base
for the architect's decisions. The program materials prepared for these purposes are the educational specifications."[11]

Educational specifications may, however, serve
other valuable purposes. They may, for example,
serve as a stimulus to cooperative curriculum improvement involving administrators, school staff,
and central staff, with the specifications being
a summarization of such work. They should define
existing educational programs and point out desired
future programs for the spaces to be constructed.

All too frequently a school administrator
accepts the first design solutions of the architect, or under duress of time, accepts slight
modifications of previously constructed facilities as the basic design. Educational specifications should reflect the educational program of
the school and be developed in such a manner that
they definitely serve the purpose of providing the
architect with a guide that interprets the educational program for the new addition or remodeled
spaces. Providing the architect with a statement
of educational function for the facility with all
the activities listed is also a prime component
of educational specifications.

How are educational specifications developed?
Educational specifications developed by a planning
team should result from a three-step procedure
which:

1. Describes the education program (courses, services, etc.) to be housed in terms of activities, process, the clientele, equipment, and materials used. (Ultimately, of course, all of these elements find their justification in the desired educational outcomes.)

2. Relates the program explicitly to basic factors of school planning.

3. Communicates these relationships to the architect by means of the written and spoken word, illustrations of relationships, and by a continuing exchange of ideas between educator and architect as the educational specifications are transposed into architectural plans and specifications.

All planning team members must be encouraged to use all means to express ideas relative to the program considerations and requirements. In order to do the most effective job of writing educational specifications, attention should focus on details of instruction and space requirements. Anything the team considers to be important for the program description should be included in its report. It is better to over-explain or define in excessive detail than to omit ideas of importance in a report to the architect confronted with a design problem.

Educational specifications are based on a great deal of data. It is not an overly difficult task for the amdinistrator to assign to each of the team members the responsibility of supplying specific data. Once each has collected data assigned and put it into readable form, then the team can share and organize the complete written package.

What data are required? A complete facility must obviously accommodate the program as it exists at the time of initial occupancy. It must also continue to serve the program as it evolves in the future. For these reasons, information is needed about the present program, and also comparable information about the program as it is envisioned in the future.

It may help in the planning team's deliberations, prior to reporting the information called for, to reflect on the purposes. Just what are you trying to accomplish? What kind of product do you expect to achieve? Answers to these questions will determine the shape of the program. Planning team members should be urged to think beyond the limit of the present building, program, and methods.

Seeking answers to the following specific questions may help in the building of a set of educational specifications:

1. How would you describe the desired student outcomes in terms of competencies--i.e. skills, knowledge, attitudes?

2. What kinds of experiences are likely to facilitate gaining these competencies?

3. How might these experiences be best organized--in scope and sequence?

4. What new developments in content and/or method may affect the future program?

The following is suggested as a guide for preparing a written statement on educational specifications. Each part should be assigned to the team member most qualified to provide the ideas or materials. Each item is important for its contribution to the complete planning cycle.

Guide for Preparing Educational Specifications

1. Describe courses and/or special experi-
    ences to be taught in the new facility
    or addition.

2. Specify the competencies students com-
    pleting these courses should possess.
    What skills should they have? What
    knowledge should they possess? What
    attitudes should they exhibit?

3. Describe time and scheduling patterns
    to be used in the facility.

4. Identify special grouping of students
    and other arrangements within each
    class or section. The manner of
    grouping should be compatible with
    the type of instruction taking place.
    Thus, if the primary function is to
    disseminate information, the basic
    section may consist of a large group
    of 25 or more. If interaction is
    also desired, small groups of no
    more than 15 students might compro-
    mise the first level of subdivision.
    Finally, individual research and study
    might call for an additional level of
    subdivision. If sections of the courses
    are to be subdivided, indicate in detail
    how this is to be done, including the
    extent to which time is a factor in
    such grouping.

5. What specific activities will take place
    in each course or experience and what
    materials and movable equipment will be
    needed for each?

6. What type and amount of permanent equip-
    ment must be present within an instruc-
    tional area to accommodate the activities
    described in the answer to question five?

7. Describe the materials that need to be stored in teaching and learning areas. Give specific size in height, depth, and width.

8. What new instructional strategies or technological developments (in content and/or method) may affect learning experiences in the future (i.e., what major trends should the educational specifications take into account)?

9. What problems relating to student traffic, if any, affect school operations?

10. What problems relating to the utilization of audio-visual materials and equipment are likely to be encountered?

11. Describe unique acoustical problems that must be solved to permit optimum instruction, particularly in such areas as music rooms and shops.

12. Describe unique illumination problems that must be solved to permit optimum instruction, particularly in mechanical drafting areas or instructional materials centers.

13. What unique thermal environmental considerations (temperature, humidity, etc.) must be solved to permit optimum instruction?

14. What learning areas demand special access treatment to permit optimum instruction, that is, what areas (such as kindergarten) require outside doors as well as corridor entrances?

15. What unique utilities requirements are needed for what courses?

16. What are the audio-visual requirements for instruction?

17. What are the special furniture and equipment requirements for each instructional area?

18. What kinds of spaces will teachers need for instructional preparation?

19. What other unique considerations deserve attention such as: carpet for all floor areas, rear screen projection capability, teachers' lounge, outdoor-indoor teaching space, special communication wiring and sound treatment, special outdoor environmental education areas?

20. What space relationships should exist? For example, what learning activity should be located next to or nearby what other learning activity?

21. What space relationships should exist within specific instructional areas? Planning team members should think in terms of daily class activities, the methods, the materials, and the equipment that have been asked about in the previous questions.

A sketch of the area may be useful in the preparation of educational specifications. The sketches of the planning team need not be concerned with size, shape, scale or accuracy for that is the challenge which confronts the architect and is the area where the architect has the greatest skill.

Sketches of the following instructional spatial area relationships are often useful in planning:

1. Student work areas including the location of chairs, desks, tables, work benches, small group stations, etc.

2. Location of storage spaces for materials that should be accessible to students.

3. Location and shapes of storage for student work.

4. Arrangement of teacher work stations showing placement of desks, preparation areas, etc.

5. Design of storage for materials used primarily by teacher or only under close teacher supervision.

6. Location and amount of chalkboard, tackboard, display areas, A-V outlets.

7. Convenient location for utility services.

8. Location of areas for delivery of materials.

Planning team members may use triangles, circles, hexagons, blocks, squares, or whatever desired to prepare instruction area sketches. They should in no way be concerned with a high degree of precision that approaches a finished architectural design. Discourage school staff team members from preparing drawings of precise scale or design of a space. The architect will reflect the thinking of your sketches when providing the building design.

When all of the educational specifications guide questions have been answered, then all the data must be combined in readable form. The educational facility consultant usually is the person designated to assume this task. If the planning team does not have the services of an educational facility planner, then the administrator will have to designate how the job will be accomplished.

The number of copies of educational specifications to be printed will vary. All planning team members should have at least one copy. The architect requires three or four for his staff. A

superintendent should have enough for certain
members of his central staff and a copy for each
board member. The administrator will want enough
for his/her staff. If the bond issue for construction of a new addition or remodeling has not
been approved, then enough copies should be available for lay groups or organizations. The size
of the educational specifications report is not
fixed. It should be as long as is necessary to
tell the architect the story which will enable
him to design a functional facility for learning.

After the architect receives the educational
specifications report, it is his responsibility
to develop the design of the facility according
to the requirements of the specifications. Another
major use of the written educational specification
is to evaluate the architect's preliminary and
working drawings in light of how well he has provided for the mandates of the report in his facility design.

The concept of developing and writing educational specifications for architects is not new.
However, the development and use of educational
specifications for new facilities, additions to
buildings, and remodeling of facility areas has
not been widely used as a facility planning procedure by administrators. Probably one of the reasons
for minimum use is that few educators have taken the
time to go through the process. Or, perhaps the
concept of what written educational specifications
look like and contain is not clear.

The chapter that follows presents illustrations of written educational specifications for
particular features of a senior high, middle
school, and elementary school.

SUMMARY

The administrative position in education is
confronted with many and varied responsibilities.
This volume is concerned with only one set of

leadership challenges, namely those related to the administrator's role in designing, utilizing, and managing the educational facility. It is written from the point of view that the school plant is the largest piece of instructional equipment and has a major influence on most, if not all, aspects of the teaching-learning process. Functional school plants do not happen. Planning is essential to increase the chances of the facility design being conducive to the achievement of quality learning environments.

The unique focus of this volume is on the administrator. Most volumes on school facility design write from the vantage point of other specialists in educational facility planning, design, construction, and management. Planning is a complex process and is future oriented. It demands allocations of time and supporting resources, and calls for the establishment of a planning team at the attendance center level where the administrator serves as chairman and where personnel who constitute the prime users of the facility are also involved. Early in the planning stages an architect and educational consultant are needed to work with the planning team at the building level. The model of the dynamic relationships among the members of the facility planning team is indicative of many formal and informal interactions among team members. A team approach was proposed because a school plant is much too complex for one person to have all the expertise needed to design a functional facility.

The basic approach of this volume is to review the educational facilities from the standpoint of environments conducive to learning that are to be generated through the planning process. Among these environments are the visual environment, thermal environment, acoustical environment, and aesthetic environment. All have an influence on the program and the instructional process.

Educational specifications serve as a concise and comprehensive guide to the architect. Without development of the educational program and its spatial interpretation, a "Procrustean bed" may be created instead of a functional school plant. If the school facility is to be an instrument important to the educational program, then it must be designed to be more than a shelter house. A planning team is necessary to stipulate the spatial demands of a set of curricular offerings and instructional strategies. In spite of frequent demands for preparation of careful educational specifications over the last decade or two, educational specifications have not been employed to the degree that is desirable. Probably one of the reasons for minimum use is that few educators have taken the time demanded to complete the process. The administrator and his/ her planning team are key personnel in the preparation of a set of educational specifications to guide the architect in the development of a functional school concept.

NOTES

1.   C. Theodore Larson, ed., <u>School Environ-</u>
ments Research Project 1: Environmental Abstracts
(Ann Arbor: Architectural Research Laboratory,
University of Michigan, 1965), p. 375. Used by
permission.

2.   Council of Educational Facility Planners,
Guide for Planning Educational Facilities (Columbus,
Ohio: The Council, 1969), pp. 113-132. Used by
permission.

3.   Ibid., p. 128.

4.   W. Bruce, <u>Man and His Thermal Environment</u>
(Ottawa: National Research Council, Division of
Building Research, 1960), p. 1. Used by permission.

5.   Dr. Charles Peccolo, <u>Thermal Environment</u>
and Learning (Iowa City: Iowa Center for Research
in School Administration, University of Iowa, 1963),
p. 10.

6.   T.C. Gilles, <u>Thermal Energy Usage at</u>
William E. Orr Junior High School, Las Vegas,
Nevada (Palo Alto: Lennox Industries, Inc., 1968),
p. 1. Used by permission.

7.   Bettye Johnson, "A Study of Color in the
Classroom Environment," (Ph.D. diss., University
of Tennessee, 1963).

8.   S.J. Knezevich, "A Procrustean Bed or Functional School Plant," American School Board Journal (November 1961). Used by permission.

9.   Ibid.

10.   John Dewey, Dewey on Education: Appraisals, Reginald Archambault, ed. (New York: Random House, 1966). Used by permission.

11.   James D. MacConnell, Planning for School Buildings, copyright 1957. By permission of Prentice-Hall, Inc., Englewood Cliffs, N.J.

CHAPTER II

EDUCATIONAL SPECIFICATIONS

AT WORK

The previous chapter stipulated that functional school plants rest upon a base of careful planning. One of the end products of the planning process is a set of educational specifications. If Procrustean beds are to be avoided, educators must insist that educational specifications be submitted as the prelude to architectural planning. The specifications represent the ideas of planning teams headed by the administrator.

It was implied that there are procedures to be followed and special consultants who can help the prime users of a facility to participate more effectively in the planning of school plants. To be useful guides to action, the specifications must be in sufficient detail. Illustrations of the type of detailed information demanded will be presented in this chapter. A complete set of educational specifications for a school facility often is a sizable document. This book cannot present complete building plans. The following application of the ideas to an instructional materials center for a senior high, the so-called unified arts area for a middle school, and an art room and administrative center for an elementary school are taken from actual plans for illustrative purposes.

THE HUNTER HILL RESOURCE CENTER

The school in question is called Hunter
Hill. The staff and the administrator recognized that the existing library area for the
high school was too small to meet the instructional needs of the school. The administrator
requested the superintendent to review the
facility needs and support the request for an
addition to the building or at least some remodeling to provide a materials resource center
to replace the small and inadequate library.
The superintendent referred the issue back to
the administrator and staff for development of
specifics on improvements to the existing buildings. This was another way of asking for a set
of educational specifications for the space in
question.

The administrator often is not quite sure
what the details of a better material resource
center would look like even though the inadequacies of the present facility were felt by
the entire staff. This stimulates the formulation of a planning team to include school staff
members such as the high school librarian, the
library's prime users, and knowledgeable persons
outside the building such as other school librarians, department chairmen, the state department
of education's educational facility planner, the
state department of education's library consultant, the district assigned architect, a university resource consultant, and a representative
from the superintendent's office. After several
meetings the group agreed that because of limited
funds, planning should be directed toward remodeling a large study hall area. This would be more
realistic than an addition to house the instructional materials resource center.

With the several policy decisions approved,
the planning team assignments were made. Within
a few weeks the following written educational
specifications were developed to solve their

particular problem of providing an instructional resource center for the school. It is important to realize that decisions made in planning are based on existing conditions and the input that is made available for the planning team. The specific steps in developing an instructional material resource center for the Hunter Hill School may deviate from those submitted in the previous chapter. Nonetheless, the general approach can be applied. The educational specification guide and report are necessary prior to the architect's design for a remodeling.

The following is the Hunter Hill's planning team's solution to developing specifications for remodeling the large study hall area to serve as an instructional material resource center. Remember that this report was developed primarily for the architect to be used as facility design information. Note that an educational rationale introduces and supports the definition of spaces that follows.

Educational Rationale

The Hunter Hill High School program endeavors to provide a rich and diverse set of learning opportunities for the wide range of individual needs, interests, and abilities found in the modern school. To achieve this goal all resources, both material and human, must be utilized to the fullest extent.

Important additions to our knowledge and new instructional strategies are evident to many educators. Current practices such as team teaching, programmed instruction, flexible scheduling, computer-assisted teaching, and individualized curricula are illustrations of changes in the ongoing process. They necessitate a careful examination of the tools of teaching currently in use and of the ways in which they relate to the programs of instruction. To illustrate, large group presentations enable the teacher to use a wide variety of illustrations, demonstrations, and visual aids hitherto impossible in small group presentations. Teaching teams working closely in the planning and presentation of all phases of work in their special area will require a greater variety and number of resource materials if they are to do an effective teaching job. It is equally important to provide comparable resources for small groups and for individuals who may work at various ability and interest levels.

It would be unrealistic to assume that a teacher or team of teachers could generate the professional planning and materials needed for the effective presentation of such programs without adequate clerical assistance, material aids, library resources, and planning time. Spaces must be provided for such purposes as well.

The materials used in teaching and learning are so many and so varied that no teacher can possibly know all about them, even in his own field, much less attempt to acquire, handle, and store them for classroom use. A centrally located instructional materials resource center (IMRC) that would combine the library, audio-visual, and student and teacher work areas seems to be the answer for the educational program as it is developing in the Hunter Hill School.

A well-planned facility, providing a wide range of materials along with devices for assisting teachers and students in the selection, preparation, and use of these materials can enhance the improvement of educational opportunities available at Hunter Hill High School.

The center should be developed for the use of all departments within the Hunter Hill High School. All the activities to be carried on in it are as diverse as the area itself. Fully developed, it will be the nerve center, the core, the heart of all learning activities of the school. The use which teachers and students make of this resource center will influence, in part, the quality of the educational program.

IMRC Missions

The following is a general statement of educational missions for the planned Hunter Hill High School Instructional Materials Resource Center. This center is only a segment of the entire school plant, but it has the potential of enriching all phases of the educational program. The following statements indicate the types of spaces or areas within an IMRC that will enable it to fulfill educational objectives.

1. By providing a laboratory area for student research and study, Hunter Hill will help students learn to think and study independently as well as in small groups.

2. By allocating areas where collections of instructional materials can be housed, Hunter Hill will be in a better position to meet the interests and abilities of every student in the population who frequents the library and IMRC Center.

3. By introducing students to a variety of instructional materials, the IMRC will help them to be discriminating users of printed and audio-visual materials.

4. By providing a greatly expanded IMRC facility, students will be given an opportunity for cumulative growth in library skills and development of reading, listening, and viewing abilities and tastes.

5. By making available a diversity of materials within an IMRC, Hunter Hill

faculty will be in a better position
to stimulate the use of the library
during and after school hours.

6. By providing an IMRC with a rich
store of reading materials, the
faculty will be better able to stimulate and guide students in all phases
of reading so students may find increasing enjoyment and satisfaction
in their lifelong experiences.

7. By designing a more functional IMRC,
the teachers will have a better means
of making students aware of the role
of the school and public libraries
as social institutions and the part
they play in the community.

8. By designing a more functional IMRC,
there will be additional books and
materials that enable the teacher to
design many varied learning strategies.

9. By making additional IMRC space available, it will be possible to have an
area for housing materials for continuing professional growth of the
school staff.

10. By providing an expanded IMRC, students
and staff will find a better place to
go for study, relaxation, and leisure
reading.

Orientation and Space Relationships

An instructional materials resource center
has many aspects. Each special dimension will be
considered independently. For purposes of summary,
the major components are listed as follows:

A. Library Resource Center, which includes:

1. circulation desk, office, and
   work area
2. book stacks
3. research area
4. small group research area
5. recreational reading area
6. independent student study carrels
7. audio-visual materials and equipment storage area

B. Teachers' Preparation and Audio-visual
   Preview Center, which includes:

   1. teachers' research area
   2. teachers' workroom
   3. audio-visual preview area

Space Utilization

The present study hall area provides about
3,800 square feet of enclosed space which can be
converted into an instructional materials resource
center. Subject to revisions and allowances, the
following space allocations for various functions
are proposed:

		Space Allocations (sq. ft.)
A.	Library Resource Center	
	1. circulation desk, office, and audio-visual materials equipment area	300
	2. library area (stacks and reading)	1,600
	3. students' independent study and small group study areas	1,000
	Total	2,900

B. Teachers' Preparation and
Audio-visual Preview Center   <u>900</u>

Total Space for IMRC   3,800

Detailed information in the design of spaces
follows:

A. Circulation Desk, Office, and Audio-
visual Equipment Storage Area

1. Traffic flow

a. The circulation desk should be
placed so as to allow the librarian or clerk to view most
of the stacks, study cubicles,
and research room.

b. All traffic from the corridor
or from the independent study
student areas should pass or
be controllable from the circulation desk.

c. Teachers or students moving
from the library area to the
upstairs teachers' preparation
and preview area should also
pass the circulation desk,
which will be the distribution
point for AV materials as well
as for books.

2. Furniture, storage, and equipment

a. Metal or wood are the suggested
structural materials to be used.

b. A stool 30" high should be at
the circulation desk.

c. 30" x 60" desk with chair is
needed for the office behind
the circulation desk.

-52-

d. Three additional chairs.

e. A minimum size of 4' x 6' tackboard.

f. Three legal size file cabinets.

g. Section of bookshelves approximately 12 linear feet.

h. Films and filmstrips will be stored in commercially manufactured cans which are then placed on a storage rack.

i. One counter for audio-visual equipment storage.

3. Utilities

a. Lighting must be adequate to meet library standards (65-75 foot-candle at desk level).

b. Duplex 110 volt A.C. electrical outlets should be on all walls of office.

c. One electrical 110 volt A.C. outlet is needed at book check-out stand.

d. A water source and sink is desirable in small work area.

e. A phone is requested for the office.

4. Visual, thermal, and acoustical considerations

a. Visual treatment--lighting to meet library standards of 65-75 foot-candles at desk level.

Color and general decor should
reflect a feeling of warmth
and dignity. There should be
no glare confronting any reader.
The surfaces of all desks should
be light in color to enhance the
brightness balance.

b. Thermal considerations are the
same as for the balance of the
school with mechanical ventilation and local control of heating and cooling.

c. Acoustical treatment should meet
highest library standards, which
includes carpets as well as special ceiling treatments.

B. Library Book Stack Area

1. Traffic flow

a. Traffic into the library should
enter through a corridor into a
single main entrance.

b. Traffic can be expected to be
fairly uniform throughout the
day with no peak periods. Large
classes will seldom arrive at
the library "en masse." Students
will work independently, utilizing
the library frequently but irregu-
larly.

c. The library book stack area will
be primarily a book depository;
hence this area should have only
a few research tables. These
are for temporary use rather than
for long study periods. Students
will go to the card catalog, to
the stacks for brief browsing, and

then to the independent study
carrels or recreational reading area.

d. Some teacher traffic will come
from the teachers' preparation
area upstairs.

2. Furniture, storage, and equipment

a. Since the furniture of the
library is in a sense both
furniture and storage space,
these items will be reviewed
under a common heading.

b. Metal is the suggested basic
structural material to be
utilized.

c. The number of book stacks
should be estimated at not
less than ten books per student.
This means at least 5,000 books,
but the number might well rise
to 7,500 in a relatively short
period of time.

d. One linear foot of shelving holds
about eight average size books,
so that at least 875 linear feet
of shelving are necessary.

e. No span of book shelving should
exceed three feet. Shelving
should vary in size from 8" to
10" in depth and there should
be at least 12" clearance between shelves. Shelves should
be adjustable if possible.

f. Stacks should be no more than
six shelves high.

g. At the end of each row of stacks it would be well to have a 24" x 36" table with one straight chair.

h. A free-standing magazine rack that would hold up to 25 current issues of magazines.

i. A newspaper rack with ten holders.

j. The card catalog file should be sufficiently large to hold the indexing system. With the necessary guides, 1,000 cards per tray would necessitate 24 trays. Each should be capable of being removed from the catalog file.

k. A reference table 2' x 3' is requested, with book rails at the ends and across the back to hold the Readers' Guide to Periodical Literature.

l. Three legal size three-drawer files are needed for pamphlets and looseleaf fugitive materials.

m. The following items should be placed near the IMRC entrance:

> Two sections of tackboard of 4' x 6' size
> One locked glass display case of 4' x 6' size

n. The reading circle for recreational reading should be treated quite differently from the balance of the library and should contain the following furniture:

Two large couches
Three or four occasional
  chairs
Suitable coffee and lamp
  or end tables

3. Utilities

    a. One refrigerated drinking
       fountain should be in the IMRC.

    b. Several duplex outlets for 110
       volts A.C. are requested for the
       recreational reading area.

    c. Overhead lighting should provide
       at least 65-75 foot-candles at
       desk top level throughout the
       library. This becomes a severe
       problem in the book stacks where
       shadows frequently reduce light-
       ing levels.

4. Visual, thermal, and acoustical
   considerations

    a. The lighting requirements should
       meet library standards.

    b. Color and decoration should contri-
       bute to a dignified environment
       and desirable brightness balance.

    c. Color and texture treatment should
       be directed toward making the li-
       brary a most desirable place to
       work and study.

    d. Thermal problems are similar to
       those in the balance of the school
       plant. Particular attention should
       be given to the probability of
       noisy heating and ventilating units.
       Local control of ventilation, heat,

and cold should be provided.

e. Acoustically, this area should be treated with care. A library is not necessarily a place where complete quiet should be maintained, but sharp, disturbing noises should be controlled. Movement back and forth always creates a certain amount of background noise which is not disturbing if kept within reasonable bounds by acoustical treatment, which includes carpets and drapes.

5. Special requirements

Aisles between stacks and doors leading to the library should be sufficiently wide to allow passage of book carts.

C. Students' Research Room

A small group of students will work collectively in the research room to pursue projects involving some discussion and some quiet work. Large vision strips around the room should make it possible for a person at the circulation desk to observe the activity.

1. Furniture and equipment--the following are recommended:

a. Table space and seating for six to eight students

b. 4' x 6' tackboard

c. 4' x 6' chalkboard

2. Utilities: visual, thermal, and
   acoustical considerations

   a. Visual considerations--65-75
      foot-candles at desk top level.
      Color and decorations should
      enhance the appearance as well
      as the brightness balance.

   b. Thermal considerations--Proper
      ventilation should be assured.

   c. Acoustical considerations--
      Highest library standards, in-
      cluding carpeting.

   d. Special electrical specifications
      other than the previous lighting
      requirements are as follows:

         Duplex 110 volt A.C. outlets
         on each wall

D. Independent Student Study Area

   1. The total proposed program aims to-
      ward the ultimate expression of edu-
      cational maturity: independent study
      and thought. Since the library has
      limited study space, it is necessary
      to have a special area where students
      can study. To meet this end, student
      study carrels should be provided as
      part of the library resource center.

   2. Provision should be made for at least
      20 spaces in this study area. These
      spaces should have at least 25 square
      feet and should contain a carrel which
      would provide at least 2 x 3 feet of
      work space.

   3. Students should be given major respon-
      sibilities for their conduct while

working independently, according
to regulations developed by the
student government. Some inci-
dental supervision of these study
areas will be provided by a librarian working in the library
resource center which overlooks
the student study area. At least
one adult should be in each library
resource center at all times.

4. The independent study area will work
   best when both students and teachers
   realize the value inherent in students taking responsibility for their
   own conduct and learning experiences.
   Reading, thinking, planning, writing,
   and discussion of study assignments
   can take place in this area. These
   activities should occur, not because
   a teacher stands over a student and
   says, do this, but because the student
   sees an opportunity to prove he is
   ready to accept responsibility.

5. Furniture and equipment

   The following furniture should be
   supplied for the independent study
   area:

   a. 20 carrels, 2' x 3' size

   b. 20 chairs, cushioned seats and
      form-fitting backs

6. Utilities: visual, thermal, and
   acoustical considerations

   a. Minimum of 65 foot-candles of
      light at desk level with parti-
      cular caution to avoid glaring
      surfaces.

    b. Duplex outlets 110 volt A.C.
       for each carrel on the room
       perimeter or every 12 linear
       feet on perimeter.

    c. Visual specifications have
       been previously discussed; color
       and decoration should provide a
       comfortable feeling. Thermal
       considerations require the area
       to be treated to deaden background
       noise and provide an environment
       conducive to quiet study.

E. Teachers' Research and Workroom Area

   1. Traffic flow

      Teachers will enter their preparation
      area near the library circulation desk.

   2. Furniture, equipment, and storage

      This center should be provided with
      the following furniture and equipment:

        Typewriter--typewriter desk--
          typist chair
        Paper cutter
        Paper punch
        One 18" x 24" sink with hot and
          cold water
        Six foot counter with under-counter
          storage
        Copying machine
        4' x 4' tackboard
        4' x 4' chalkboard
        Ten extra straight-backed chairs
        Under-counter storage
        Six study carrels, 2' x 3' size
        Six chairs, cushioned seats and
          form-fitting backs
        30 square feet of work table space

36 feet of book shelving for
   professional library
Storage zone for coats and
   other personal items

3. Utilities

   a. Teachers' preparation center
      should be equipped with a tele-
      phone, overhead lighting, and
      duplex 110 volt A.C. electrical
      outlets.

   b. Perimeter 110 volt A.C. duplex
      outlets should be provided for
      each carrel.

4. Visual, thermal, and acoustical
   considerations

   The teachers' preparation area should
   adhere to the same specifications including carpeting as other areas of
   the instructional materials resource
   center.

F. Audio-visual Preview Area

   This space will be an integral part of
   the teachers' preparation area. Traffic
   will be light and made up primarily of
   teachers coming to preview films and tapes.

   1. Furniture, equipment and storage

      a. 6' x 6' permanently mounted
         beaded screen should be placed
         at one end of area.

      b. Storage unit of teachers' pre-
         paration area might be utilized
         as a partial curtain or divider
         to allow previewing with limited
         additional use of folding doors
         or curtains.

         c. Counter for placement of
            audio-visual equipment which
            will include movie projector,
            overhead projector, slide
            projector, and tape recorder.

    2. Utilities

        Two duplex 110 volt A.C. electrical
        outlets are required.

        A separate control should be designed
        for overhead lighting.

    3. Visual, thermal, and acoustical
       considerations

         a. Very little close work will be
            done so that 50 foot-candles of
            light will be adequate.

         b. Same heating and ventilating
            requirements as the rest of the
            building.

         c. Acoustical considerations are
            very important.

         d. The teachers' preparation area
            must be shielded from excessive
            noise that might be generated
            during audio previewing operations.

A UNIFIED ARTS FACILITY FOR HEAVENLY VALLEY
MIDDLE SCHOOL

The Educational Rationale

    The middle, intermediate, or junior high
school of America is caught up in an era of change,
partially as a result of the recent changes in
elementary education, partially because of basic
changes taking place in the comprehensive high
school, and partially due to other forces in
American society. Research discloses that learners

differ from each other in abilities, capacities, and the willingness to learn, and significantly so in the ten to fourteen year old age group. This information suggests the need for different ways of doing things with different kinds of learners.

Some forces generating change within schools for the early adolescent include:

1. The downward push of curricular experiences once believed to belong at higher grade levels, causing an increased complexity and variety of subject matter at lower grade levels;

2. The necessity of individualizing instruction so as to identify pupils who can cope with all or parts of the curriculum;

3. The universal desire to maximize instructional effectiveness; and

4. Identification of potential dropouts so as to design a program pertinent to their needs.

As indicated in previous sections, the middle school should be designed with only one purpose in mind--the accommodation of an educational program. The decision was made to make Heavenly Valley a middle school. The building must be designed and constructed so that all aspects of the program can be geared to the innovative educational techniques, free from restrictions on learning strategies imposed by unyielding physical barriers. This requires that the middle school facility design stem from a knowledge of how students learn, as well as what and how they will be taught. Therefore, planning will start with a description of the desired educational program, then proceed to a determination of the facilities needed to house this program.

Any description of the educational program of a middle school must involve analysis of the expected educational outcomes; discernible current and future trends in curriculum content; present and future class enrollments; instructional methods and materials; specific teaching and non-teaching activities; interrelationships of spaces; internal and external student traffic patterns; kinds, sizes, and amounts of furniture and equipment; utility services; visual, thermal, and acoustical needs; kinds, sizes, and numbers of storage area; and unique requirements. This description of the educational program provides the basis from which design and specification decisions may be rendered by the architect.

The middle school (grades 6-8) movement has been gaining impetus since its inception several years ago. This pattern fosters a more gradual transition period from the simple organization of the elementary grades to the complexity of high school. The rationale of this movement is the general acceptance of the concept that in a middle school the early adolescent can make a fruitful and pleasant transition from the general experiences of the elementary school to the more specific and intensive experiences of the high school. Many opportunities are provided for exploratory learnings in a wide range of fields. These changing conditions influence the educational program and the number, kind, and location of educational facilities to house the program. Through intelligent planning, change (and its bearing on education), and education (and its bearing on change) must be studied and understood.

Popper, in this organizational analysis of the middle school, defined its central goal as follows:

> "The differentiated function--hence, the paramount goal--of the American middle school is to intervene protectively in the process of education which was

begun in the elementary school, mediate
between the human condition at the onset
of adolescence and the pressures of culture, and continue the general education
of early adolescents with a curriculum
applied in a psychosocial environment
which is functional for learning at this
state of socialization."[1]

Therefore, the basic functions of the middle
school are to provide for a smooth transition
from elementary to high school; to furnish educational facilities and an educational program
suited to the growing degree of specialization
of interests of pupils at this level; to provide
exploratory educational experiences for students
to help them discover their potentials for academic and vocational pursuits; and to provide the
most efficient, effective, and satisfying relationships between the student and the school-community.

In developing programs and facilities that
focus on the characteristics of middle grade
youngsters (ten to fourteen years of age), the
school in the middle is faced with an uncompro-
mising challenge. In a three or four year period
these young learners will move rapidly through a
complex developmental cycle which will take them
from childhood to full adolescent standing. They
undergo physical, social, psychological, and intellectual changes that affect attitudes and behavior in a manner unique from either the elementary
or high school group. Finley described this age
group as "tween-age kids who are one day adults,
another day little children; some days they like
you, and other days they don't even like themselves."[2] The characteristics of this middle
age group are predictable, but on occasion exas-
perating to parents and educators alike. These
youngsters generally:

    1. Seek self-direction and self-expression
       in a world that is often puzzling, mis-
       understanding, or even hostile.

2. Model a variety of cultural roles in a search for self-identity.

3. Form a complex, idealistic value structure that evolves from childhood, adolescent, and adult frames of reference.

4. Experience irregular and often opposing emotional and physical drives.

5. Expand their interests in developing diverse talents and decision-making responsibilities.

6. Exhibit a wide range of individual performance capabilities which they cannot fully assess or appreciate.

Middle School Program Demands

The special characteristics of the middle grade student foster special educational needs that are powerful determinants of the middle school program. Some of the most important needs are as follows:

A. Basic Skills Needs

1. Communication skills--Reading, writing, speaking, and listening skills should be developed to the maximum potential of each student.

2. Critical thinking experiences-- Burton defined critical thinking as "the reflective search for valid conclusions which solve our problems, resolve our doubts, and enable us to choose between conflicting statements of doctrine or policy."3 Subsumed under this heading are inquiry and problem

solving which should be developed
in all phases of the curriculum.

3. Quantitative understanding--Students
   should comprehend the basic mathe-
   matical processes and be sensitive
   to the connections between them.
   They need skills in applying mathematics in a creative way to resolve
   the many problems that confront them.
   Traditional goals of mastery of computation and manipulative skills are
   stressed and include such elements
   as numbers and operation; geometry;
   measurement; application; statistics
   and probability; sets; functions; and
   graphs.

4. Physical development skills--The wide
   range of physical, emotional, and
   social development in youngsters ten
   to fourteen years of age requires a
   diverse program that focuses upon the
   development of a variety of fundamental body skills. The program
   should contribute to and foster the
   growth of student confidence, leadership, control of emotions through
   group relations, and enjoyment.

5. Economic understandings--The multiple
   difficulties associated with the buying and selling of goods and services
   in our complicated and fast-changing
   markets directly affect young people.
   Consumer education to develop a sense
   of value of material things and the
   rights of ownership will be a part of
   the basic skills program.

B. Exploratory Experiences

   The middle school learner needs many opportunities to explore new interests and to
   choose certain of these for more intensive

work. Each student should have the opportunity to learn enough about his interest in such areas as the following to decide whether to participate for an extended period: art, dance, drama, home arts, industrial arts, journalism, music, foreign language, student government, photography, electronics, and various occupational experiences.

C. Intercultural Experiences

The ability of individuals to get along with one another and of groups to function in a cooperative manner toward common goals is imperative for our survival. The main purpose of providing intercultural experiences is to give each child the opportunity to learn about and understand his own culture and the contributions that sub-cultures have made to the development of our society and the world.

D. Social Responsibilities

Young people need opportunities to live and work together, develop a sense of worth and belonging, and develop school-civic habits of service and responsibility. The program will provide action problems that will help youngsters understand human relationships realistically and through intersocial problem situations learn how to achieve common goals.

E. Psychological and Emotional Security

Children who are secure, confident, and well-adjusted take on learning tasks with enthusiasm and with a high probability of success. However, those who are fearful, reticent, and wary of failure are hardly

likely to face and react to problems
within acceptable limits and achieve
the goals of learning. The teacher
is the key to success--good rapport
between the teacher and student is an
essential ingredient to a healthy
learning environment.

F.   Human Relations

The need to relate to others is a
justification for a school. The fulfillment of this need demands freedom
of interaction and communication for
students within the school. The focus
is upon developing people "skills"--
ways of building positive relationships
with others that are mutually satisfying
and productive.

G.   Removal of Time Pressure

All pressure in a school is not detrimental; however, undue and indiscriminant
pressure can hinder the learning process.
Children need to have the opportunity to
interact with their peers, plan activities,
and make decisions without being forced
to keep one eye on the clock or calendar.

H.   Success Needs

Each student needs a variety of learning
experiences in which he has a chance to
succeed. Rewards for interest, efforts,
and improvement are imperative. Very
few people can experience repeated failure and develop into reasonably productive
citizens with a sense of self-worth.

I.   Privacy

A major characteristic of the young adolescent is his diverse and almost

constantly changing needs and
interests. To balance the heavy
pressure of groups, the school
should offer each student facilities and time when he can be by
himself to work or even to dream.

Program Guidelines

The educational program of the middle school
builds on the foundation provided by the elementary
schools in such basic skills as arithmetic, reading,
writing, and spelling. Concepts of science, health,
family life, the rights and duties of citizenship,
and moral and spiritual values which have been introduced in the earlier school years are broadened
and extended. A major orientation emphasis in
exploring the many components of various careers
should be initiated at this time.

The subject matter of all courses should be
planned for the maturity level of middle school
pupils and be adjusted in terms of individual
differences among the pupils as determined by the
staff. No pupil should be expected to meet a standard that is beyond his ability to achieve, and no
pupil should be judged satisfactory if his achievement is below his potential.

Design Considerations

From the previously mentioned needs and requirements of the middle school student, certain
design considerations emerge. As you develop the
middle school educational specifications, a multitude of design assumptions and considerations must
be provided for the architect to assimilate. From
there he will be able to provide the functional
aspects of the design. More detailed and pertinent
information results in the greater possibility that
the facility will ideally serve students and staff.

The following are examples of the kinds of
statements that should be made concerning the functional facility design:

Since it is the function of the building to facilitate the educational program, the middle school facility must be arranged in such a way that it will enhance each educational task of the present operation, yet be completely adaptable to other educational changes that are also destined to develop in the years that lie ahead.

The significance of change to the school plant planning process is self-evident; yet, the uncertainty of the direction of future changes demands the utmost flexibility in order to allow the planning process to be successful. Without exact information for the future, assumptions must be made and used as the basis for developing design criteria. These assumptions are based upon innovative trends that have occurred during recent years, and can be broadly classified into three areas: innovation in the curriculum, innovations in administrative organization, and innovations in physical facilities. Curriculum trends include:

1. An interdisciplinary approach to curriculum planning.

2. Teaching fewer isolated concepts and facts in the social and physical sciences.

3. Teaching more exploratory courses in the humanities and unified arts.

4. Teaching more language and recreational courses.

5. Individual student programming based on a research approach to learning.

Among recent trends in administrative organization are the following:

1. Team teaching and planning.

2. The use of teacher aides and clerical assistants.

3. The development of the flexible
   scheduling of time spent on various
   subjects and activities.

4. Flexible class sizes.

Trends in physical facilities include those
toward:

1. Planning large open instructional
   spaces free of arbitrary partition
   placement that promote flexible
   grouping, resource flow, and planned
   spatial reorganization.

2. Increased use of multi-functional
   furniture, electronic equipment, and
   audio-visual hardware.

3. Compact design.

4. More concern with environment--carpeting,
   air conditioning, acoustics, and aesthetics.

Adaptability, Flexibility, and Expansibility

The program dimensions should influence design and construction. A program statement deserves highest priority in the planning of all
new middle school facilities. The necessity for
consideration of educational factors cannot be
stressed too much, from both the perspectives of
long-term adaptability and the short-term flexibility. Without doubt, the content of the school
curriculum and the teaching strategies that accompany it during the next fifty year period will
make it highly desirable to rearrange interior
spaces and utility services in a way to permit
the size and functions of each teaching station
to be changed.

Short-term flexibility allows almost daily
manipulation of space dividers, that is, the kind
of flexibility that permits modifications of

arrangements in a classroom or other space on almost a moment's notice. Such flexibility might be nothing more than rearranging furniture, chairs, or other equipment and furnishings to create spaces for different areas, or it might be achieved using mechanically or electronically operated partitioning.

Long-range adaptability refers to providing for easy remodeling or expansion. In providing this type of flexibility, the following characteristics should be given consideration:

1. Open-end corridors

2. A compact plan

3. Good site utilization

4. Non-load-bearing partitions

5. Grouping conduits, pipes, and ducts for ease of maintenance and change

6. Arranging spaces for community use so they are readily accessible to patrons

7. Mechanical and electrical systems zones to serve separate areas

8. Flexible and convenient storage units

9. Movable furniture and equipment

10. Maintenance-free exteriors

The physical plant must provide the right kinds of spaces for the program. Two points that must be kept in mind during the planning of this school are flexibility and expansibility. Modular coordination should be considered as a means of obtaining the greatest possible economy in space utilization and future expansion.

A significant problem connected with flexibility is that there is no guarantee that the partitions available today will be available at the time of future expansion, hence the great need for the use of component parts of standard sizes. Constantly evolving programs must not be limited and hampered by the inflexibility of fixed spaces.

In addition to the above, special consideration must be given to writing design implications for the thermal, acoustical, visual, spatial, and aesthetic environment; community use; the use of all kinds of electronic and equipment aids; communication and safety systems; storage; teacher space requirements; basic student space and equipment requirements; outside environment treatment and non-professional staff work space and equipment.

Considerations of Space Requirements and . Functions

It is necessary in writing the middle school specifications, as it is for the elementary and secondary school, to provide data concerning facility space relationships, square footage requirements, and a description of space functions and special considerations for any instructional space adaptations. A complete set of educational specifications for a middle school would be a sizable document. The general material described in previous paragraphs could apply to many such attendance centers. For purposes of illustration only one type of instructional space will be detailed. The following is an example of what specific facility requirements might be for a middle school unified arts area. This particular unified arts area was developed to accommodate a studentbody of some 1,000 middle school students.

UNIFIED ARTS AREA

The middle school will house a comprehensive program that enables all students to gain an appreciation of the values of an aesthetic experience while, at the same time, acquiring the skills basic to effective daily living in our complex and dynamic society. To offer a program of such scope, it is necessary to provide a cluster of highly specialized spaces in which the unified arts program can be accommodated. The unified arts program has four major goals:

1. To utilize and reinforce many concepts and skills learned in the academic subjects, i.e., math, science, language, and social studies.

2. To provide the opportunity to work with a wide variety of materials and tools.

3. To encourage open-ended inquiry through a rich variety of exploratory experiences.

4. To provide the opportunity to relate the unified arts to such significant technological and social problems as mass production, product design and quality, research and development, raw material utilization, safety, and communication.

This area could be one of the focal points of the middle school plant and will integrate visual arts, exploratory technology, homemaking and consumer education, and commercial education. These disciplines are largely activity-oriented and should take place in laboratory environments. The entire unified arts area can be viewed as a laboratory in which students investigate and employ many skills and media of a similar nature. They require special equipment, similar service requirements, and many similar safety provisions. These considerations have led to the recommendation that facilities for visual arts, exploratory technology, homemaking, consumer education, and commercial education be grouped together.

The interdisciplinary nature of these disciplines requires more than just physical training facilities. Each major laboratory area and the various sub-areas should be blended together to produce an environment which stimulates flow, creativity, and accomplishment. The open laboratories, with flexible partitioning systems, will allow for diverse activities to be carried out simultaneously, permit more adequate supervision, and encourage new approaches to evolve naturally. The free flow of materials, projects, and personnel will enable students to integrate their own experiences in these closely allied fields. Thus, the unified arts program will provide more realistic simulation of real-life experiences.

Unified arts will include the following major areas and sub-areas:

A. Visual Arts Center

    1. Painting laboratory
    2. Crafts laboratory
    3. Storage

B. Commercial Education Center

    1. Business laboratory
    2. Graphics laboratory

C. Exploratory Technology Center

    1. Construction and fabrication laboratory
    2. Power and electronics laboratory
    3. Storage

D. Homemaking Education Center

    1. Foods and nutrition laboratory
    2. Clothing and textile laboratory
    3. Family living laboratory

E. Resource Center

F.   Gallery

G.   Staff Center

General Requirements

1.   110 and 220 volt power provided in each
     laboratory area. Double wall outlets of
     approximately nine foot spacing around
     perimeter and not less than 48 inches
     from the floor.

2.   Main electrical panel for equipment and
     receptacles in each laboratory, with
     control switch and pilot light on the
     outside of each panel.

3.   Room lights controlled from the entrance
     to the classroom and laboratory area.

4.   Gas lines to have one main shutoff valve
     in each laboratory.

5.   Hot and cold water to be included in each
     laboratory.

6.   Room clocks, tied into the master system,
     for each laboratory.

7.   Heating, ventilating, and air conditioning
     must be ducted separately from the rest
     of the complex.

8.   Ceiling heights to be determined by
     equipment used (hoists, monorails, etc.)
     as well as ventilating equipment.

9.   Drinking fountains to be included in each
     laboratory.

10. Floors which must support heavy equipment
     and supplies must be throughout, except
     where otherwise noted.

11. Floors should be hard-finished, slip-proof, and sound-absorptive through-out, except where otherwise noted.

12. Fire extinguishers, fire blanket, and alarms to be installed in accordance with local codes.

13. Sinks and student cleanup facilities required in each laboratory area.

14. Provisions for A-V, TV, audio, and inter-com systems in each laboratory area.

Specific Space Allocations and Functions for the Unified Arts Laboratory

The detailed capacity, square footage, and description of functions and special considerations for each instructional activity in the unified arts area can be found in Table 1. The specific information is necessary if the architect is to design functional spaces relevant to the instruc-tional needs of a unified arts program.

HAPPY HAVEN ELEMENTARY SCHOOL
ART AND ADMINISTRATION CENTER

This is the third illustration of part of a set of educational specifications. The previous two focused on secondary education facilities. The following applies to an elementary school plant.

Educational Rationale

The design and construction of new elemen-tary school buildings must be arranged in such a way that they will enhance each educational task of the present operation, yet be completely adapt-able to educational changes that are also destined to develop in the years that lie ahead.

Educational specifications for school facili-ties grow out of a stated philosophy and curriculum

TABLE 1. Specific Space Allocations for Unified Arts Area--18,450 square feet total.

Type of Space	Unit Capacity	No. of Units	Total Area (in sq. ft.)	Description of Functions and Special Considerations
1. Visual Arts Center			3,500	Activities will include two and three dimensional work that includes instruction in drawing, painting, sculpture, crafts, ceramics, and related activities.
				Center is open with distinction between painting and crafts laboratories largely functional, not physical.
				Provide outside patio adjoining laboratories.
				Special consideration must be given to floor surface in this area. Acoustical qualities must be retained and at the same time, the surface must be easy to clean and maintain.
a. Painting Laboratory	24	1	1,500	This area to serve as an all-purpose or multi-discipline two-dimensional art laboratory for individual and small group projects. Equipment in this area shall be flexible and interchangeable to enable students to work on projects in any of the following subject areas: basic art, drawing, or painting.
				This area to have a considerable amount of tackboard surface for display of two-dimensional art work. To be provided around perimeter of room and by use of space dividers with tackboard surface.

Type of Space	Unit Capacity	No. of Units	Total Area (in sq. ft.)	Description of Functions and Special Considerations
a. Painting Laboratory (continued)				Student drawing tables are to be flexible and movable to allow students to work on individual or group projects in painting, drawing, or basic art. Tables will not be used for storage of drawing boards or student projects. Provide space and equipment for a painting studio including an area for model or still life setup with special lighting effects.
				Provide art storage cabinets in lab that include units capable of storing paper stock up to 36 inches wide; also provision for individual storage facilities for each student, e.g., tote tray storage.
				Provide adequate artificial lighting throughout.
				Perimeter counter sinks with hot and cold water required throughout.
b. Crafts Laboratory	24	1	1,500	This area to serve as an all-purpose or multi-purpose discipline three-dimensional art laboratory for individual and small group projects. Equipment shall be flexible and interchangeable to enable students to work on projects in any of the following subject areas: ceramics, sculpture, and crafts.
				Considerable amount of three-dimensional display area required with special accent lighting effects. A portion of the display area should be secured. Portable space dividers can also serve as three-dimensional display units.

Type of Space	Unit Capacity	No. of Units	Total Area (in sq. ft.)	Description of Functions and Special Considerations
b. Crafts Laboratory (continued)				General storage required for materials, supplies, and equipment used in ceramics, sculpture, and crafts. Must include bins for storage of clay, plaster, etc. Provide storage for student projects in process including wet ceramic storage area with temperature and humidity control. Include student apron storage.
				Student work benches are to be flexible and portable to allow students to work on individual or group projects in ceramics, sculpture, or crafts. Tables to be designed so that they may be grouped around special service centers containing sink, cold and hot water, air, and gas which are to be located throughout the area. Sinks must have plaster traps.
				Provide electrical outlets for two kilns. Include exhaust about kilns.
				Include equipment typically used in crafts projects such as potter's wheels and spray booths for ceramics, weaving equipment, and hand saw for sculpture.
c. Storage		1	(500)	General storage required for art supplies and equipment. Provide drawing board storage and painting drying racks. Include temperature and humidity control and ample shelving for clay storage.
2. Commercial Education Center			2,800	Provide an introduction to clerical, business and commerce concepts, commercial use of graphics, and journalism.
				Carpeted throughout except in graphic arts laboratory.

Type of Space	Unit Capacity	No. of Units	Total Area (in sq. ft.)	Description of Functions and Special Considerations
2. Commercial Education Center (continued)				
a. Business Laboratory	24	1	(1400)	Semi-open area throughout with acoustical isolation of typing area.
				Basic furniture consists of bookkeeping desks and chairs.
				Provide electrical connections to all student stations for variety of electrical machines, e.g., typewriters, adding machines, etc.
				Equip with peripheral casework counter top with storage facilities, counter level electrical outlets, and sink. Also provide individual tote tray storage.
				Provide area for checkout counter, display counter, and clerks.
				General storage for materials and equipment.
b. Graphics Laboratory	24	1	(1400)	Multi-purpose laboratory to enable students to work on projects in photography, lettering and layout, printing, illustrations, and drafting.
				Relate to Visual Arts Center and Exploratory Technology Center.
				Provide various types of student work stations including drawing tables, layout tables, light tables, etc. Equipment is to be movable. Sink units with hot and cold water required throughout area. Photo studio required and equipped for special lighting effects.

Type of Space	Unit Capacity	No. of Units	Total Area (in sq. ft.)	Description of Functions and Special Considerations
b. Graphics Laboratory (continued)				Graphics lab to be used for preparation of school newspaper. Equip accordingly.
				Secure general storage required. Also include student projects storage. One 75 square foot area should be walled off and used as a darkroom.
3. Exploratory Technology Center			4,500	An open multiuse area for work with woods, metals, plastics, electricity, and small engines. Lab identification more by function rather than physical separation.
				Provide sub-area identification by work bench arrangement, machinery location, freestanding visual screens, and some demountable floor-to-ceiling partitions.
				Ceiling should have exhaust ducting for fumes and dust. Individual exhaust ducts provided for each woodworking machine.
				All machinery securely mounted; include safety guards where necessary.
				Each lab to be provided with compressed air.
				Remote control off switches for all machines. Panic buttons in three locations.
				Relate labs to outside exit for ease in supply delivery.

Type of Space	Unit Capacity	No. of Units	Total Area (in sq. ft.)	Description of Functions and Special Considerations
a. Construction and Fabrication Laboratory	28	1	(2200)	Activities include work with wood, masonry, painting, plumbing, paper hanging, metals, plastics, and welding.
				Provide individual perimeter work stations in addition to four-place group work areas. Equip with lockable perimeter cabinets that permit project storage.
				Tool storage will be provided by wall-hung storage facilities and movable tool carts.
				Include small paint booth with compressor.
				Provide dust-free drying area.
				Provide hot metals area for welding activities.
				Provide project planning and storage areas.
b. Power and Electronics Laboratory	28	1	(1800)	Allows exploratory work in the areas of electricity, instrumentation, radio, television, air-conditioning, and engines.
				Provide perimeter work area for individuals in addition to four-place small group work spaces.
				Provisions for wall-hung tool storage and space for movable tool carts.
				Provide hood exhausts for small gas engine area.
				Dust control in electronics area.
				Provide project storage.

Type of Space	Unit Capacity	No. of Units	Total Area (in sq. ft.)	Description of Functions and Special Considerations
c. Storage			(500)	Storage and preparation of raw materials for labs.
				Provide doors wide enough to permit ease of supply movement and storing of tool carts. Equip with movable shelving for storage of supplies.
				Provide heavy adjustable perimeter shelving for large items, e.g., electronic equipment, motor parts, and heavy metals.
4. Homemaking Education Center			3,700	Introduction and exploratory experiences related to general homemaking activities. Relate to exterior exit for delivery.
				Entire area should be designed with a domestic quality and be aesthetically pleasing and inviting.
				Entire area to be open. Only special functions isolated.
a. Foods and Nutrition Laboratory	24	1	(1400)	Area should include six complete kitchen-dining units designed to look like a home kitchen-dining area with double sink, range and oven, refrigerator, garbage disposal, dishwasher, and dining table. Include additional work tables that can be functionally grouped.
				Stain-resistant floor covering.
				Special consideration to ventilators.
				Instructor's demonstration table and overhead mirror shall be portable.

Type of Space	Unit Capacity	No. of Units	Total Area (in sq. ft.)	Description of Functions and Special Considerations
a. Foods and Nutrition Laboratory (continued)				Storage of canned and dry cooking items should be in area that can be locked but easily accessible for distribution to cooking stations. Provide tote tray storage.
b. Clothing and Textile Laboratory	24	1	(1400)	Provide seven 4' x 8' tables of height convenient to 10-13 year old students with enclosed tote tray storage to be provided if table bases have insufficient capacity.
				Furnish 14 sewing stations with electrical power available to each.
				Zone a private grooming area with counter, three-way mirror, electrical outlets, special lighting provisions, and counter/top sink and water. Also zone an area for ironing boards and electrical outlets for irons near grooming area.
				Provide one clothes washer and dryer. Include laundry sink.
				In addition to general storage include student project storage, ironing board storage, wardrobe storage, and bins near laundry area for soiled clothing.
c. Family Living Laboratory		1	(900)	Typical efficiency apartment to be used for instruction in furniture arrangement, cooking, social hospitality, apartment decor, etc.
				Space to include living room, kitchen, bathroom, bedroom, utility room, and storage room.
				Storage area should be directly accessible to apartment (minimum 100 square feet).

Type of Space	Unit Capacity	No. of Units	Total Area (in sq. ft.)	Description of Functions and Special Considerations
c. Family Living Laboratory (continued)				Direct access to foods lab, clothing lab, and main traffic circulation.
5. Resource Center	30	1	1,500	This area to serve as a unified arts resource and study area.
				Locate central to the four main instructional centers. Should be designed around learning mall concept, combining circulation and resource center functions.
				This area will provide transition from main circulation and IRC and Unified Arts Center.
				The student furniture in this area will consist of reading tables and study carrels interwoven between the home-type lounge furniture and book shelving. The study carrels will be equipped with AC electrical duplex outlets and audio-visual terminal units.
				Low level book stacks, not over 42" high, will be included in this area for storage of enrichment materials relating to this area, including reference books, dictionaries, trade magazines, textbooks, audio-visual material such as slides, filmstrips, cassettes, tapes, records, etc., and all other resource matter.
				A browsing area should be included here with comfortable lounge type furniture and shelving space for magazines and periodicals.

Type of Space	Unit Capacity	No. of Units	Total Area (in sq. ft.)	Description of Functions and Special Considerations
6. Gallery		1	800	This area will be the main display area for all unified arts activities.
				The total area to be designed for two and three dimensional display. In the center of the area shall be located a motorized rotating platform for display of special projects. Special lighting required for accent of display areas.
				Provide comfortable lounge type seating to create small group conversation areas.
				This area should stimulate student interest and demonstrate the interdisciplinary aspects of the unified arts program.
				This is the main circulation mall leading from main IRC to Unified Arts Center and Resource Center.
7. Staff Center			1,650	Home base for all instructors and clerical aides. Provides office space, storage, work area. Included is a general purpose conference room.
a. Office (10 @ 60 sq. ft. ea.)	10	1	(600)	Open area that is zoned by casework and visual partitions into space for instructors and aides.
b. Work Area		1	(100)	Used by instructors and aides for preparation of instructional materials. Direct access to office and storage area.
c. Storage		1	(200)	Storage of clerical supplies, books, and related items. Provide movable storage shelves.
d. Classroom	30	1	(750)	This area to be equipped as a general purpose classroom to be used by all major activities in the department.

Type of Space	Unit Capacity	No. of Units	Total Area (in sq. ft.)	Description of Functions and Special Considerations
d. Classroom (continued)				Provide folding walls to divide space into two small group areas.
				Locate adjacent to Resource Center. Design with demountable partitions that can be removed so that the classroom will be an extension of the Resource Center.
				Special consideration shall be given to the acoustics in this area because of its location in relation to the labs. Should be insulated from noises generated in the lab area.
				Students shall have easy access to the classroom area from the lab areas, as well as the Resource Center.
				Provide a service center at one end of the classroom area equipped with a sink, hot and cold water, and AC electrical power for demonstration purposes. Install portable demonstration tables for the instructor.

for elementary education. The basic philosophy
for an elementary program could include the
following:

1. The central purpose of the educational
    process is the development of each
    individual student to the maximum of
    his potential.

2. All learning takes place within the
    individual and each individual human
    personality differs in some way.

3. Students have enough similarities in
    common to make it possible for most
    aspects of the educational process to
    take place successfully in groups, the
    size of which will vary according to
    the characteristics of the educational
    task and range of interest and abilities
    of the individual.

The function of elementary specifications is
to describe the philosophy of the program, describe present and anticipated elementary school
needs in terms of functions, space requirements,
program characteristics, and design objectives.
Basic facility planning assumptions will emerge
and these must be written so that the architect
has guidelines for facility implications. Facility
planning assumptions form the foundation for developing the educational space allocations and
relationships for elementary school facilities.
The self-contained classroom approach (as opposed
to the open concept) was adopted as the basic
instructional organization for Happy Haven. A
few examples of other basic planning assumptions
are as follows:

A. The school plant should be designed to
    accommodate approximately 800 students.
    A total of 24 elementary classrooms and
    two kindergarten classrooms should be
    designed to accommodate approximately
    800 students. Instructional spaces

should be grouped around, insofar as possible, a learning center which will form the nucleus or focal point of the school. Additionally, this facility must include areas for administration, nurse, teacher lounge/work space, conference space, storage, custodian, and toilets. Note again the relationship of these factors to continuing the self-contained classroom pattern.

B. The building structure must provide adaptable and flexible space within an overall envelope of educational environment. Although it is anticipated that staff utilization and the application of flexible grouping techniques will serve as the basic instructional approach in the future, it is cautioned that the use of the self-contained classroom unit must not be ignored for the present. Hence, flexibility within the total building facility must be emphasized, and it should be possible for rooms to be enlarged or decreased in size in order that teachers may vary their practices in whatever manner thought to be best for more effective learning. Carpeting should be used throughout the school as a means of improving the educational and psychological environment, as well as for acoustical purposes.

C. Space for small group instruction should be incorporated within each classroom area. A variety of group instructional patterns fit specific kinds of learning procedures in the elementary educational programs. Pupils may move from large-group activities with team teaching to small group or individual sessions, or into any other pattern appropriate to special needs. To accommodate small groups, classrooms must be zoned for such spaces as reading corners or similar areas.

D. Spaces outside the building necessary
    to the educational function should be
    conveniently located. The building
    should be so located on the school
    site so that exterior spaces will be
    convenient. The exterior areas for
    which provisions should be made include
    physical education and play, and vehicu-
    lar parking and service areas. Physical
    education and play areas should be loca-
    ted so they are directly accessible from
    classrooms, and the area for kindergarten
    should be separated from the elementary
    grade level area. Parking areas pro-
    vided for the public, staff, and visitors
    should be conveniently located and may be
    combined.

There could be as many as 30 to 40 basic
planning assumptions with facility implications
developed for the educational specification document. The above example depicts the planning for
a closed classroom concept. In the last chapter
of this book the open-space school concept is
discussed with facility implications.

The administrator and his team must determine
the general elementary program chacteristics for
the new facility. They can be described in a
variety of ways. One approach is to utilize
subject matter areas and describe them by stating
educational outcomes, discernible trends, and
activities. The following is an example of how
this might be arranged for the area of art.

Art

A. Educational Outcomes

    1. To manipulate and explore, indivi-
       dually and in groups, a wide
       variety of art media and tools,
       thereby developing imagination
       and coordination.

-93-

2. To gain security, satisfaction, and pleasure through self-expression in art media.

3. To express visually individual thoughts, feelings, and ideas.

4. To develop creative ability, thereby satisfying spiritual and aesthetic growth.

5. To observe, understand, and appreciate design in nature, art, and everyday living.

6. To develop skills for occupying spare time enjoyably and profitably.

B. Discernible Trends in Art Instruction

1. Greater use of audio-visual media.

2. More emphasis on design and imagination in all art activities.

3. More stimulation and guidance from teachers.

4. More experimenting with a wider variety of materials.

5. More emphasis on arts and crafts as a leisure-time activity.

C. Student Activities

1. Drawing and painting, using wax crayon, colored chalk, and water and oil paints.

2. Sculpturing and carving.

3. Linoleum, woodblock, and silk screen printing.

4. Collage.

5. Textile printing.

6. Molding clay and plaster work in ceramics.

7. Use of copper, plastic, and aluminum materials.

8. Papier-maché

Summary of Art Activities

Art activities may be closely integrated with other classroom work. The activities will include work in the regular classroom as well as in a special area. Each teacher should have basic art supplies readily available in his immediate complex. These basic materials would include scissors, paste, crayons, chalk, paint, brushes, sponges, and a supply of assorted papers. The basic supplies should be readily accessible so as to make it easy for the teacher to conduct the integrated art program.

Art easels should be available and they should be portable. Ample display space should be provided in all areas of the lower-school complex. Permanently fixed sections of chalkboard and tackboard are less desirable than flexible sections that can be moved in and out with little difficulty. A varied crafts program will also be a part of art instruction and a separate area will be needed for this work and for storing supplies for each classroom complex.

After the assumptions and general program characteristics have been developed and written, then the following information should be developed for each art facility space.

1. The expected occupancy of each area.

2. The approximate square footage of each area.

3. A description of the primary activities and purposes for which the area
should be designed.

4. Description of major furniture and
equipment requirements which relate
to space.

5. Appropriate general considerations for
each area and space.

6. Simple drawings showing the general
relationships within and between areas
of the school facility.

Elementary School Administrative Offices

An example of how the above information might
be developed is shown in Table 2 in a description
of a possible elementary school administration
area relationship.

The information should be as detailed as
possible so that the architect can provide the
design that will accommodate all the requirements
of each space. Providing the kind of information
as shown in the example is essential for all
spaces within the proposed elementary facility.

With the above information, and with the
district's educational philosophy, its program,
and the relationships which should exist between
the school's programs and the facility, the architect should be prepared to design the appropriate
facility.

MOVING INTO THE NEW FACILITY

An in-service program for staff utilization
of the new facility or building addition is a
perennial but to date unsatisfied need. The
administrator must accept this leadership responsibility as a very important step in facility
planning.

TABLE 2. Specific Space Allocation for Administration Center--3,100 square feet total.

Space	Maximum No. of People	No. of Units	Total Area (in sq. ft.)	Description of Functions and Special Considerations
1. Principal's Office	4	1	150	The principal's office is primarily his workroom where he plans the operation of the school, carries on study activities which promote the general welfare of the school and community, visits with parents and patrons, confers with staff and students, and from which he communicates with those agencies most important to educational planning and programming.
				Relate to public entrance and teacher traffic via public waiting and school secretary.
2. Auxiliary Offices	4	2	150	Space to accommodate activity of transient instructional/guidance personnel.
				Relate to public entrance and teacher traffic.
3. General Office	2	1	300	This area is used by teachers, pupils, parents, and other visitors who desire to see the principal or his assistants, or who may need the secretarial services of this office.
				Relate to public entrance and provide a comfortable, cheerful, welcoming atmosphere which encourages students, teachers, and visitors to freely come and go from the office area.
				Provide two secretarial stations. Also provide casework display for lost and found articles.

Space	Maximum No. of People	No. of Units	Total Area (in sq. ft.)	Description of Functions and Special Considerations
3. General Office (continued)				Provide direct access to exterior circulation, principal's office, health suite, bookroom, and conference room.
4. Health Suite	3	1	300	Space for health conferences, individual hearing tests, first aid, and work space for the nurse.
				Provide sink with hot and cold water.
				Relate to general office and provide control by school secretary.
				This room should provide for three areas: (1) examination area; (2) rest area; and (3) toilet room and shower.
5. Bookroom	--	1	350	Central supply and book storage space for entire school and work space for the administration complex.
				Controlled access from general office area.
6. Conference Room	25	1	500	Utilized for group conference with parents, teachers, etc.
				Desirable to divide into two smaller spaces by use of operable wall.
				Direct access from general office.

Space	Maximum No. of People	No. of Units	Total Area (in sq. ft.)	Description of Functions and Special Considerations
7. Staff Lounge and Workroom	30	1	1,100	To serve dual purpose of teacher work space and lounge. This space should be divisable by use of movable furniture and equipment.
a. Workroom Area				Direct access to Learning Center.
				Casework cabinets along two walls with counter top; one wall section to be extra depth.
				Furniture to include large work tables (4' x 8') and chairs.
				Teacher mailboxes to be located in this area.
				Counter sink with hot and cold water.
				Provide utilities for electric 220v kiln and shelves for storage of ceramic models and materials.
b. Lounge Area				Furnish with casual chairs and sofa.
				Locate community kitchen equipment in this area. Equipment to include counter top sink with hot and cold water and extra elevated faucet for filling coffee urn, 10 cu. ft. or larger refrigerator, counter top burners. (Domestic stove and refrigerator may be substituted.)
8. Faculty Toilets		2	250	Separate toilet facilities should be provided within the complex for men (50 sq. ft.) and women (200 sq. ft.).
				Relate to teacher workroom and outside workroom circulation for access.
				Sink units to be supplied with hot and cold water.

Years ago most faculties could move into a new facility and encounter minimal problems of space utilization. Practically all schools were designed in the same way. Mainly, there were classrooms to accommodate 25-35 students and the teaching method primarily included recitation, lecture, and reading activities.

Today, we find a real change in many new facility designs. Spaces are developed for small group, large group, and individual learning activities. Large interior open spaces have replaced the rigid 25-35 student classroom structure. Small resource center areas have been developed for math, history, science, English, and other discipline areas. Much of the equipment is mobile with the capability of being used in many ways.

If the teaching staff is not made cognizant of the flexible possibilities of the new facility, then the old design should have been constructed. The staff will normally use the new building just as they did the old one unless an in-service program is provided for facility utilization.

The physical size of the facility and size of staff will determine the length of time required for a facility familiarization program. An administrator should first work with his/her department chairmen and administrative and supervisory staff to plan for the scheduling of student and teacher utilization of spaces. When this has been accomplished, the architect, educational consultant, department chairmen, and other administrative staff should make decisions about how the various spaces in the facility can be best used to provide a very profitable learning experience for all students. Here the educational consultant and architect can be of great help to the administrator and his key staff members as space utilization consultants.

For example, one of the first problems that is normally encountered when small resource spaces are provided for various areas of the facility is the fact that many librarians are hesitant to allow library books and AV media to be dispersed to other areas of the building. This is foreign to the normal procedure followed in the regular centralized approach to use of resource materials.

A plan of action must be worked out concerning distribution, accounting, and use of books and materials from the central library to the small resource areas. This procedure must be accomplished before staff and students move into the new facility, or the librarians, teachers, and students will revert to the previous concept of going to the central library area for materials and the valuable small resource areas will not be stocked and become wasted unused spaces.

When decisions have been made by the administrator and his key staff members, with advice from the educational consultants and architect, on the best space utilization plan for the new facility educational program, it is time for an in-service program for all staff members. The actual time for an in-service program will vary. Enough time should be allotted to ably describe and show all staff members how the new facility should be used for student learning experiences.

An effective approach to facility orientation and use is to train a demonstration team of teachers to show others how furniture, equipment, and spaces can be arranged to encompass a variety of learning activities. After the facility orientation program, following movement of the staff and students into the new facility, a follow-up observation should be undertaken by the administrator and his supervisory staff to see if suggested space utilization techniques have been undertaken.

When a teacher or teachers are observed making exceptional use of space, equipment, or furniture, this should be brought to the attention of other staff members. Only through constant encouragement to use the facility as it was planned to be

-101-

used will the majority of staff members change
their concept of how teaching space should be
utilized.

SUMMARY

The Hunter Hill Instructional Materials
Resource Center educational specifications described some of the major space concerns for such
a center. Other information could be provided
on functions and activities of spaces by students
and teachers. However, it is a general outline
and does provide sufficient direction for developing more detailed educational specifications.

Educational specifications can be as simple
as the illustrative sets outlined or be developed
in much greater detail. The major purpose is to
establish written and vocal communication with
the architect so that the most functional design
will be developed for the money allotted.

An architect would take the educational
specifications at this point and start to develop
his sketches and preliminary drawings to establish
a workable interior design for the proposed senior
high school Instructional Materials Resource Center,
the middle school Unified Arts Area, or the elementary school Administrative Area.

The planning team must view the architect's
sketches and preliminary drawings in light of how
well they relate to the statements and demands of
the educational specifications. The architect
should be able to quote line and page of the
specifications to defend the design features of
his preliminary drawings. If the preliminary
drawings are not directly related to what was
stated in the specifications, then the planning
team should refer the architect to the educational
specifications and request that the preliminary
drawings be redesigned. The above situation could
occur because: (1) the educational specifications
were not specific or detailed concerning what were
to be the functions of the educational facility;

or (2) the architect had many preconceived ideas about what the design should be and did not bother to interpret the educational specifications into the desired functional design model.

Development of useful educational specifications and interpretative dialogue between the planning team and the architect's team is essential for quality facility planning. Illustrations were provided for aspects of a senior high, middle school, and elementary school. First a rationale was proclaimed, then more specific missions of the facility were outlined, and finally detailed space allocations and functions were described.

Moving into a new facility is a challenge to the administrator. A period of in-service development may be needed to realize the full potential of a new facility.

NOTES

1. Samuel Popper, The American Middle School:
An Organizational Analysis (Watham, Mass.: Blais-
dell, 1967).

2. Dr. Robert M. Finley, "The Middle School,"
a report to the Board of Education, Glen Cove, N.Y.,
November 18, 1968. Used by permission.

3. William Burton, Washoe County School Dis-
trict Middle School Educational Specifications
(Reno: Research and Educational Planning Center,
University of Nevada, 1971).

CHAPTER III

LEARNING TOOLS: INSTRUCTIONAL

EQUIPMENT AND FURNITURE

Greater emphasis on individualized instruction and educational innovations, in general, places increased importance on a greater variety of instructional equipment, furniture, and supplies that facilitate individualization and innovation. This trend expands the responsibilities of the administrator for planning and design. Whereas paper, pencils, and textbooks used to be sufficient for the student's classroom activities, this is now no longer the case. There appears to be a never-ending demand upon the school, elementary and secondary, for specialized furniture; a variety of supplies such as scissors, rulers, pencils, paper, simple maps, plus the very complicated programs and sophisticated computer equipment for computer-assisted instruction laboratories.

The shell of the building including air conditioning, carpeting, and the rest of the mechanical and electrical design components will make up from 65-75 percent of the new facility budget. The remaining 25-35 percent is directed toward providing furniture and equipment for student, staff, and administrative use. An important task for the administrator in planning for a new facility or an addition to his/her building involves the decision concerning selection of furniture and equipment.

There are many ways to buy furniture and equipment for new facilities, remodeled areas, or new additions to a building. The administrator can duplicate the furniture or equipment that is a part of his present school or other schools in the district. This is not always the best solution, particularly if presently owned district furniture leaves much to be desired in terms of function. Replicating past mistakes in the new facility leaves much to be desired and should be avoided.

Some administrators may seek the most inexpensive instructional tools as a response to a very limited budget. Buying the cheapest may result in early maintenance and breakage problems which, in turn, lead to higher operating costs and minimum efficiency of use. Prudence dictates examining other than the most obvious alternative. It makes good sense to confer with other administrators to gain their experience on purchasing instructional equipment and furniture in their new facility. Opinions of teachers and students may be the source of other good ideas about the advantages and disadvantages of existing furniture and equipment. One thing is certain--teachers, as well as department chairmen, should be asked to provide recommendations concerning the kinds and shapes of furniture that would fit their program activities.

Developing furniture and equipment specifications for the architect is valuable. Knowing the size, number, and shapes of furniture and equipment provides him with a tangible problem of arrangement that can be solved with the right design. Information from staff, students, architect, other administrators, and equipment and furniture industry personnel can provide enough information to state furniture and equipment needs for the new addition. The written specifications for equipment and furniture for the new addition or remodeled area do not have to be complex. They should identify furniture, equipment, and casework items needed to expedite the educational task within your facility. From this information, architects and others may be aware of the possibilities and limitations of the

furniture and equipment units involved in a set
of specifications.

No specific brand identification should be
made or implied nor exact measurements quoted.
The intent should be that the decor of a particular unit's form and function be described so that
architects and school officials may freely choose
the specific brand items that each occasion demands under purchase bid conditions. Table 3 is
a sample furniture and equipment specification
developed for a biology lab. The example shown
in Table 3 could serve as the pattern for listing
and describing furniture and equipment needs for
all spaces in the proposed new school or new addition or remodeled areas.

Be sure to check and double check that your
furniture and equipment requests will meet the
requirements of your learning activities. Equipment vendors or furniture and equipment manufacturers are happy to offer assistance by providing
information for decisions about furniture specifications and layouts. Some companies will prepare
a complete layout of all furniture and equipment
for each space with color and cutouts as part of
their customer service. No single company can
provide all instructional furniture and equipment
requirements for a new school. Good practice
demands collecting information from a variety of
equipment and furniture sources.

GUIDE FOR FURNITURE AND EQUIPMENT SELECTION

The following are guidelines for selection
decisions:

1. Will furniture and equipment provide
   efficient functional use for program
   activities?

2. Are floor glides on legs made of stainless steel? How do they work on the
   floor covering specified in the new

-107-

TABLE 3. Biology Lab Furniture and Equipment Requirements

Number	Description	Special Considerations
3	Table, life science, four place	Provide gas and electrical service to teach four place student station; no sinks to be provided at student station.
28	Chair or backrest stool Pupil trough sink Wet-table, 6-8 feet long	Trough sinks and wet-table to be located along each sidewall--lab sinks to be located on side and back walls.
4 1 1	Sink, small, lab Garbage, disposal unit Stool, teacher	
	Work counters and storage cabinets along walls (Check educational specifications for detailed storage requirements.)	Storage and display cabinets to be included in laboratory casework.
1	Table, demonstration (teacher)	Teacher demonstration table to include: 1) Water, gas, and electrical service; 2) Master switch to electrical outlets on lab tables; 3) Master valve to lab table gas outlets; 4) Demonstration table to include a fixed section approximately 32" x 96" with one movable section (cart) approximately 32" x 36"; 5) One demonstration overhead mirror for student observation of teacher demonstrations.
2	Wastebaskets, 16" x 16"	
1	Aquarium display window	Locate aquaria in central preparation room.

facility? Do they make marks and
noise on floor when moved?

3. Is furniture designed and constructed
   to maximize student comfort and minimize fatigue?

4. Can furniture and equipment be purchased in a variety of heights and
   sizes?

5. Is teacher's desk high enough so an
   adjustable stool can allow the teacher
   to demonstrate or lecture from a stand-
   ing-sitting position much like a drafting table and chair? This will add
   great comfort and reduce physical
   fatigue for the teacher throughout
   the day.

6. Are chairs for students stackable to
   allow for quick changes in uses of the
   room or for storage? Chairs that can
   be stacked will provide easier cleaning
   for the custodians.

7. Consider how easy it is to move so-called
   movable equipment. Try moving it on
   carpeted floors.

8. Check on sturdiness of furniture and
   equipment. How does it hold up under
   use? Does the paint chip off easily?

9. Consider separate chair and table instead of combination or arm table types.

10. Check on how easily and functionally
    tables can be fitted together to provide
    small discussion group areas.

11. Stipulate in your bid specifications
    that a sample of each piece of furniture
    bid upon accompany the bid.

12. Consider the style and color scheme for room compatibility.

13. Will storage casework actually meet the storage demands of the specified room or space to be served by the casework? Try storing all the materials, articles, and books that will be used in the classroom that need storage.

14. Are working surfaces of furniture and equipment durable and easy to clean?

15. Is furniture and equipment capable of multiple use? This is an important feature to look for. Flexibility of furniture and equipment use can be a great space saver.

The specification and selection of furniture and equipment is many times left solely to the discretion of the architect. If he does not have direction from the poeple who are going to use, clean, maintain, and supervise the use of furniture and equipment, then the administrator cannot feel with any assurance that the furniture and equipment needs of the new addition will be met in a functional and practical manner. Written furniture and equipment specifications are essential to provide the desired seating and working area for students and teachers. These provide information that is so necessary for the architect to formulate a furniture and equipment design that will bring about a perfect marriage of form and function.

EQUIPMENT STORAGE AND MAINTENANCE

In the previous chapter, reference was made to storage requirement information in the educational specifications. Of all the problems of facility design that have been encountered by school people, the one that is most common is that of providing adequate and useful storage for equipment and supplies within the new facility.

In many instances, storage requirements have been treated with little or no regard in the total design of facilities. With the trend toward more and more equipment, it is imperative that the architect be directed to the necessity that specific equipment must be stored in or near particular space areas.

Many teachers in schools today do not fully utilize the variety of technological devices and equipment available to them. One of the major reasons for not using the instructional equipment to its full potential is the fact that it is usually too far away from the teaching space and too difficult to move.

When planning for new schools, consider the possibility of providing wall mounted screens that allow an easy set up when using filmstrip, film, or slides. A controversial and expensive approach to solving audio-visual problems is provision of rear screen projection with three or four classrooms served from one central projection area manned by an audio-visual specialist. It would then be possible to utilize many teaching devices at one time in many classrooms upon the demand of the teacher. This would allow the teacher greater flexibility and would leave the machine operation to the technician who is trained for that kind of support work.

In many schools overhead projectors have been provided for teaching space. When the staff member is through using the projector, an available storage space should be close by so that the equipment will not interfere with the next activities of the teacher and students.

One storage problem that has been sticky over the years is found in the elementary school. What is the best way to store elementary students' coats, hats, overshoes, lunches, etc.? An elementary school teaching space is often organized and designed to provide a beautiful and efficient learning situation except for the clutter of

-111-

students' outdoor coats and jackets. If the architect is made aware of this storage problem, a workable solution can be found.

Another demand for storage that is often overlooked in design both for the secondary and the elementary school is book and material storage for student and teacher. Today's trend is toward providing book collections in various learning areas of the schools. There are a variety of portable book storage possibilities. However, if they are not requested for use in a designated area, the books will probably be stacked on the teacher's work area, floor, or in an inconvenient storage space.

Music and Science Storage

Very special consideration should be given to music and science storage. Unique and odd-shaped pieces of equipment and supplies abound in both areas.

Musical instruments must be protected when not in use. Many times it is necessary to utilize a locking system for the storage area. There are special requirements for storing and cataloging the many music books and sheet music that are utilized on the elementary as well as the secondary level.

Science equipment, like the music equipment, requires special treatment. When it is not being used, storage in a safe and sometimes locked area is essential. Science supplies, in many instances, are dangerous to the person not familiar with their particular characteristics. Therefore, a locking storage system is needed.

To insure that the right storage system is provided for the above special areas, the administrator should require from responsible staff personnel a list of the number and size and description of all articles to be stored. Unless the architect has the detailed list of equipment and supplies that require storage, his storage design will continue to be a guess.

SUMMARY

Instructional tools are increasing in number and complexity. They command a sizable portion of the facility's budget. Duplicating past mistakes should make administrators wary of simply copying furniture specifications of existing facilities. Specification for furniture and equipment should be developed with the help of others. The specifications should be in the detail necessary to assure getting what is desired. Furniture and equipment manufacturers will be happy to work out alternative solutions to furniture and equipment requirements at no cost.

CHAPTER IV

SCHOOL FACILITY

UTILIZATION AND CARE

In most school systems the administrator has the primary responsibility for the utilization and care of the building. Utilization of a facility by staff and students is the key in determining the student capacity enrollment figure.

SCHOOL CAPACITY

The first step in determining pupil capacity is related to the nature and functions of a school building. One's concept of a school building influences estimates of the number of pupils to be satisfactorily housed. To illustrate: If a school building is looked upon as just a shelter from the weather, many youngsters can be placed within a given space before it is over capacity. On the other hand, if a fundamental purpose is to facilitate the instructional process, the number of pupils who can be placed within a given space without crowding will be different. The school building surrounds the pupils and teachers for a purpose. Crowding interferes with the realization of this purpose. The educational program thus has an important bearing on the measurement of the pupil capacity of a building.

And again, the pupil capacity of a building changes with a significant change in the educational program or curriculum, even though the physical facilities remain constant. To illustrate:

-115-

Assume the educational program is to be limited to the three R's, and that the school building for this program has a capacity of 200 pupils. The capacity of this building would change and overcrowding would result, if the educational programs were expanded to include instruction in home economics, industrial arts, and physical education, each of which requires specialized equipment and spaces. Unless additions were constructed, existing classrooms would have to be changed from general-purpose instruction to home economics or industrial arts or physical education. Enriching educational programs without additional spaces will, in most cases, reduce the pupil capacity of a building.

The reverse of this step is often seen. Overcrowding has been relieved by reducing educational opportunities. Thus, kindergartens have been closed or moved so that the rooms might be used as primary classrooms. Art and music rooms have been converted into general purpose classrooms, and experiences in art and music thereby reduced or carried on elsewhere. The nature and extent of the educational program housed within a given school building must be agreed upon before student capacity can be determined.

Overcrowding and Adequacy

It is necessary to differentiate between the overcrowding of a school building and its adequacy. "Overcrowding" is a quantitative description, while "adequacy" is a qualitative description of the educational or physical aspect of a school building. A building is not overcrowded simply because no space provisions are made for such educational opportunities as industrial arts, fine arts, music, speech, physical education, and the like. However, a building without the just mentioned educational spaces, particularly at the secondary level, is less adequate for what is presently agreed upon as a desirable program of educational opportunities. A difficulty in measuring pupil capacity stems from the failure to distinguish between the adequacy of spaces to facilitate the desired program of education and the actual number of pupils that can be satisfactorily housed for that program.

To evaluate the usefulness of a school building, three separate measures are needed. One measure is based on the rated pupil capacity for a given educational program. The second measure is an index of educational adequacy and is based on the number and design of educational spaces necessary to facilitate a desirable curriculum for children of elementary or secondary school age. A third measure would indicate the physical condition of the structure, the site, and service systems.[1] Structural soundness, sanitary facilities, fire hazards, the quality of natural and artificial lighting, etc., are not considered in the first attempts to determine pupil capacity.

Let us examine some fundamental assumptions underlying the measurement of the pupil capacity of an elementary school, which includes grades kindergarten through the sixth. An elementary school may be organized along departmentalized, semi-departmentalized, self-contained or non-graded lines. The problem of computing the pupil capacity of the building for an elementary school organized in the "self-contained" classroom system is relatively simple. Here the pupil capacity is a function of the pupil-station standard and the area of the general purpose classroom where learning experiences take place. The pupil-station standard is simply the area allotted each pupil enrolled in a class and is the foundation of estimates to determine overcrowding.

The pupil-station standard is usually stated as so many square feet allotted to each pupil. The real difficulty occurs when a decision must be made as to what value should be assigned to the pupil-station standard. For many years, this standard for elementary classrooms was based on the floor area required for a single desk arranged in a pattern, plus enough spaces for aisles needed for circulation. The standards for primary pupils were less than those for intermediate pupils because of the smaller size of the primary desks. In the 1920's one famous architect specified that the pupil-station standard for grades 1, 2, and 3 was approximately 12 square feet per pupil; for grades 4, 5, and 6 a little over 14 square feet per pupil; and for grades 7 and 8 approximately 16 square feet per pupil. Later it became accepted that 15 square feet was the desirable pupil-station standard for elementary schools.

More recently, writers and architects point out that the classroom learning activity should influence the pupil-station standard. This is a functional development of the school building as a means of facilitating the instructional process. As teaching methods have become more and more concerned with pupil activity, educational space large enough for freedom of movement and for large student projects has become as necessary as space for furniture and aisles. Movable furniture has made it possible to arrange students in the various patterns which the learning situation demanded. Once the desk has been made movable, it can be arranged in a circle, a square, etc. This flexible arrangement of furniture makes it necessary to provide at least 25 square feet per pupil. An additional ten square feet per pupil or more are required for instructional procedures involving pupil activity. Accordingly, 35 square feet per pupil in a regular elementary school classroom should be provided as a pupil-station standard. Numerous authorities recommend a pupil standard of 20 to 35 square feet; the majority urge in the neighborhood of 30 square feet per pupil. Special classrooms, such as kindergarten, require more space.

No research at present indicates the superiority of one pupil-station standard over any other as far as instructional efficiency in the elementary school is concerned. Clearly then, decisions must be made on the evaluated pupil standard considered desirable for the program in hand and the methods of instruction.

To say that a building is at capacity without specifying the pupil-station standard is to be guilty of vagueness. To illustrate: Assume an enrollment of 500 children in an elementary building with ten general purpose classrooms, each with an area of 900 square feet. Is this building overcrowded? If the pupil-station standard of 15 square feet is accepted, the capacity of each room is 60 pupils. The total pupil capacity of this building with ten rooms is then 600 without crowding. If, however, the standard of 30 square feet per pupil is accepted, the capacity of a room with 900 square feet of area would be 30 pupils. The total pupil capacity of this ten room building would then be 300. If 200 additional pupils are enrolled under the latter assumption, then the building is operating at 167 percent of the capacity.

It is the writers' contention that there is more overcrowding in present school buildings than is known, simply because the pupil-station standard is far lower than is desirable for efficient methods of instruction.

Special Purpose Rooms

The preceding method is valid only if the pupil is in the same room under the supervision of a single teacher for a major portion of the day. If special teachers are available to "enrich" the program, it is assumed that when the children go to the special purpose room with a special teacher the general-purpose room remains vacant. It is argued that the elementary children need the guidance of a single teacher most of the day and that departmentalization confuses them. Special purpose rooms are not included in determining the pupil capacity of a non-departmentalized elementary building. Where children remain under the supervision of a single teacher during most of the day, the special purpose classroom is an extension of the general purpose classroom. The library, auditorium, gymnasium, art room, science room, music room, speech room, shop, and so on are in a sense parts of the general classroom, separated from it for convenience in the placement of equipment and efficiency in instruction. The justification for not including the special rooms in the computations of pupil capacity of an elementary school rests upon the space implications of a particular concept of elementary education. It is not based on solid objective principles but rather upon a philosophy of education. In such elementary schools a special measure of determining overcrowding in special purpose rooms during one period is needed.

In the secondary school, as well as the departmentalized elementary school it is not necessary to provide a general purpose room where a child must be located during most of the day. The special purpose rooms in a departmentalized school must be examined under a different set of educational beliefs. In a departmentalized organization, pupils work under several teachers during the school day. In addition to that, each pupil is allowed some freedom in the selection of subjects to be studied. Since the high school student circulates from one room to another during the course of the school day, the length and number of instructional periods during the school day are important elements in the determination of the pupil capacity of a secondary building. Conflicts in class scheduling must also be given consideration here when determining pupil capacity.

Influence of Program on Capacity

The formula for the determination of the student capacity of a secondary school plant cannot help but be complex because the educational programming at the secondary level is complex. If the program of all high school students were rigidly prescribed and constant, with all students at a particular grade level studying the same subjects, a definite relationship would exist between total enrollment and pupil capacity of a school plant. Were this true, schools with equal enrollments would require the same number and kinds of instructional units. But when the students are permitted to select their programs of studies, the educational program becomes a variable in the computation of pupil capacity. The writer has found in one of two schools with equal enrollments 22 class sections devoted to the study of English and social studies, and only 15 sections in this same area in the other. In the one school system, 92 percent of the students were enrolled in social study subjects, whereas in the other only 56 percent were enrolled. Schools have different graduation requirements and use different systems of counseling; even where total enrollments are equal, the number of sections in given subjects will vary. Table 4 is a description of different student requirements of two high schools in the same district.

One cannot simply examine an empty building to arrive at its pupil capacity. The same educational plant will have two very different rated pupil capacities when used for two different educational programs. The varying space demands for secondary school subjects are to a large extent responsible for this condition. Most authorities agree that a desirable standard for general-purpose or interchangeable secondary-school classrooms is 25 square feet per pupil. On the other hand, 40 square feet per pupil is regarded as the minimum for home economics. Pupil-station standards for shops vary from 40 square feet to 75 square feet or more. Some standards for physical education spaces specify at least 100 square feet per pupil for a class of average size. This variety of standards serves to emphasize that the same educational plant will have different rated pupil capacities under different educational programs.

Once again, an illustration: In the future it may well happen that fewer pupils will be interested in certain learning experiences. Thus, the shift may be from the study of home economics which requires at least 40 square feet per pupil to subjects which require only half of that unit floor area. An increase in pupil capacity would result as the number of rooms with large pupil-

TABLE 4. Enrollment Analyses

Subject Area	High School No. 1 (1,455 students)		High School No. 2 (1,518 students)	
	No. of Students	% of Total Population	No. of Students	% of Total Population
Arts--Crafts	257	17.66	240	15.81
Business	847	58.21	655	43.80
English--Speech	1,360	93.47	1,490	98.15
Foreign Language	485	33.33	570	37.54
Homemaking	290	19.93	167	11.00
Industrial Arts	495	34.02	342	22.52
Mathematics	546	37.52	605	39.85
Music	178	12.23	155	10.21
Physical Education	502	34.50	1,067	70.28
Science	973	68.87	945	62.25
Social Studies	912	62.68	1,033	68.05
Driver Training	376	25.84	110	7.24
Study Hall	219	15.05	386	25.42
R.O.T.C.	139	9.55	170	11.19
Special Education	75	5.15	---	---

station standards was reduced, hence more pupils could be housed.

Instructional Periods and Capacity

The number of instructional periods during the school day has a pronounced effect on the pupil capacity of a school. The capacity could be increased too if the instructional units were available for eight or nine instead of six periods per day. To illustrate: Assuming that a particular room accommodates 30 pupils, and the plant operates at 100 percent utilization, 180 pupils could use the room during the six-period day, while 210 pupils could use the same room during a seven-period day. Table 5 provides data on teaching stations required for a six, seven or eight period day. Note that seven or eight period days certainly can make some difference on the facility capacity.

The length and number of class periods should be based on educational considerations, particularly educational methodology. If the lecture method is used, there is some justification for periods of less than fifty minutes. Laboratory methods of instruction necessitate class periods of 50 minutes or more for effective learning. Clearly then, class period lengths should be determined by efficient instructional methods and their time requirements rather than by pupil-capacity computations. Physical education instructors desire longer periods because of the time spent in dressing and showering as well as in learning activities. Much the same is true of home economics, shop, and science subject fields requiring 50 minute or longer class periods for efficient instruction.

Scheduling Conflicts

Conflicts in scheduling classes hinders 100 percent utilization of available spaces. It is unrealistic to assume that every room in a secondary school building can be used every period of the day. Allowances must be made for flexibility in programming. Eighty-five percent utilization is a justi-

-123-

TABLE 5. Teaching Stations Required for 6-7-8 Period Day
(Based Upon 85% Capacity)*

	6 Period			7 Period			8 Period		
	Schedule Periods/Week	Teaching Stations	Adjusted Training Stations	Schedule Periods/Week	Teaching Stations	Adjusted Training Stations	Schedule Periods/Week	Teaching Stations	Adjusted Training Stations
Art	26*	3.20	4	30*	2.77	3	34*	2.45	3
Business	26	9.25	10	30	7.64	8	34	6.73	7
English	26	15.22	15	30	13.19	13	34	11.64	12
Foreign Language	26	5.60	6	30	4.86	5	39	4.28	4
Home Economics	26	3.20	4	30	2.77	3	34	2.45	3
Industrial Arts	26	4.80	5	30	4.17	4	34	3.68	4
Math	26	6.40	7	30	5.52	6	34	4.87	5
Science	26	10.41	11	30	9.03	9	34	7.96	8
Social Studies	26	10.41	11	30	9.03	9	34	7.96	8
Driver Training	26	2.56	3	30	2.22	2	34	1.96	2
R.O.T.C.	26	1.60	2	30	1.39	2	34	1.22	1
Music	--	2.00	2	--	--	2	34	--	2
P.E.	--	6.00	6	--	--	6	34	--	6
Special Ed.	--	1.00	1	--	--	1	34	--	1
Study Hall	26	3.20	4	30	2.77	3	34	2.77	3
		Total	91		Total	76		Total	69

fiable factor to use for establishing capacity for a secondary facility.

Some school buildings do not provide office space for teachers. Teachers under such circumstances are allotted at least one period a day in large empty classrooms for counseling students, planning programs, etc. In spite of the inefficient pupil-station utilization in such circumstances, this is the only way out when teachers' offices are not provided. A more efficient arrangement, of course, would be to provide special office space, to be shared by a number of teachers. If it is a school policy to use a room only five out of six periods a day, this must be recognized.

Special Purpose Classrooms

Certain rooms in secondary schools are equipped with highly specialized and relatively immovable instructional equipment for such subjects as science, home economics, industrial arts, physical education, music, art, and business education. These instructional spaces do not lend themselves to instruction in such general areas as English, mathematics, social studies, or foreign languages which do not require specialized furniture.

In determining the capacity of a secondary school plant, consideration must be given to such specialized classrooms as can be used for general purpose instruction when not in use for the originally designed purposes. To do this, however, necessitates the service of "floating" teachers who move from one specialized room to another which happens to be vacant at a particular period. The only home grounds such floating teachers would have would be a specially provided office.

Specialized classrooms do have a significant impact upon the pupil capacity of secondary school buildings. If adequate space is not provided for physical education, music, art, and vocational

areas, etc., then the general class areas will
quickly load up beyond capacity.

Year-Round School

Traditional capacity computations assume a
nine or ten month school year. If the facility
is used for eleven or twelve months, its capacity
would be extended. The same can be said for double
shift or twenty-four hour use of facilities. It
is assumed that only one student "shift" will use
the space for about eight hours of a day. If,
through staggered shifts or additional shifts,
the building is used for sixteen hours rather
than eight hours per day, the capacity would be
doubled.

In Conclusion

Any attempt to compute the pupil capacity of
a secondary school plant must consider the number
of daily instructional periods; the elective system and its influence upon pupil class programs;
the area of interchangeable classrooms and adaptable specialized classrooms; the uniqueness of
function of specialized spaces and the length of
the school year. An additional factor which
deserves special emphasis is the pupil-station
standard accepted for evaluating any and all of
the spaces in a secondary school plant. The importance of evaluating instructional spaces on
a justifiable pupil-station standard is not over-
shadowed by the complicating factors just discussed.

The complicated structure and organization
of our elementary and secondary school buildings
defies developing a rigid rule for determining
the pupil capacity of school buildings. Fundamental assumptions with respect to the nature and
extent of the educational program and methodology
of instruction must be made clear before proceed-
ing with any evaluation. There is a close relationship between the nature and extent of the educational program and the pupil capacity.

CARE OF THE SCHOOL FACILITY

If the administrator manages the custodial program within the school, then it is imperative that he/she understands the lines of authority for supervisory control of custodial personnel. Policies must be established that clearly stipulate the extent of control he or she has concerning custodial personnel in the building. If this is not established, the custodian many times will be confused by wondering who is the most important of the many masters he must serve. As a consequence, he may accomplish little and the quality of his performance may be lower than it should be. It is essential that the administrator have immediate supervision over all custodial employees in the building.

An attractive and well kept facility may be taken for granted, but it requires much hard work and planning. A building will very quickly become dirty and unattractive through use. A quality operation and maintenance program for the facility is very important for students and teachers if for no other than health and safety reasons. The upkeep of a facility over a number of years demands money for operation. Economics are critically involved in the total management of a school's maintenance program. Nonetheless, good facility operational management is necessary to make the best use of limited resources.

How do you know whether your custodial services are good, bad, or mediocre? Many evaluative approaches have been offered to help answer the above question. The one that has the greatest promise for school administrators is a quiz constructed by Feldman and titled, "How to Get Your Maintenance Program Organized."[2] This simple quiz can help you arrive at an index of the school's housekeeping operation's overall effectiveness and pinpoint specific weaknesses.

Few administrators are qualified fully to evaluate a cleaning operation without exerting special effort and time to do so. Some may be unsure as to where to start. The following custodial quiz is designed to help. Answer these simple but revealing questions. The results can help you in two ways.

First, as mentioned earlier, the results will give you an index of overall effectiveness of housekeeping operations. Being able to answer "yes" to 38 or more questions should bring on congratulations to the custodial and administrative staff. It would indicate the one in a thousand programs employing modern maintenance methods. If you cannot reach 38, your operation can stand major improvement.

Second, answering these questions can help locate weaknesses that need attention. Every question that received a "no" answer points to a specific need.

Obviously, this quiz will not solve any of your custodial problems, but it can identify them, and that is the first step.

1. Do you operate under an annual cleaning and maintenance budget?

2. In figuring your cleaning costs, do you include custodial costs, supervisory costs, cost of fringe benefits, cleaning supplies, mechanical housekeeping equipment?

3. Have you a way of comparing your cleaning costs with those of other schools?

4. Is cleaning costed out on an area or job basis?

5. Do you periodically evaluate jobs currently performed by outside contractors to see if they could be handled at lower cost by your own staff?

6. Do you periodically evaluate jobs currently performed by your own staff to see if they could be handled at a lower cost by outside contractors?

7. Have you studied current work procedures to see if saving could be effected?

8. Has full advantage been taken of the economies to be obtained by merchandising your housekeeping?

9. Do you have systems or devices for controlling the consumption of cleaning materials?

10. Have you standardized materials so that you are using a minimum number of cleaning products?

11. Do you have suitable time standards for cleaning jobs?

12. Do you have basis for comparing your frequencies of job performance with those found at other schools?

13. Do you know whether the man-hours devoted to cleaning are in line with your actual man-hour requirements?

14. Is cleaning performed on a scheduled basis?

15. Have specific performance levels been established for cleaning workers?

16. Do cleaning schedules allow for seasonal variations?

17. Do you have a system for rating levels of cleanliness?

18. Do you have written instructions for cleaning work?

19. Have definite lines of authority and reporting functions been established for the housekeeping department?

20. Are workers performing tasks other than cleaning (mail delivery, messengers, performing errands, etc.)?

21. Is adequate supervision, and relief for supervision, available?

22. Have blueprints and floor plans been used with respect to assignment of cleaning tasks?

23. Is proper training and supervision provided to any persons outside the permanent staff who are permitted to perform cleaning duties?

24. Do you have a definite plan for reduction or expansion of the cleaning force to compensate for increases or decreases in activity?

25. If a new building or wing is constructed, do you have an accurate way of predetermining personnel requirements and cleaning costs?

26. Is an effort being made to improve worker skill and efficiency through a regular training program?

27. Do your employees wear uniforms?

28. Does each worker fully understand his responsibilities?

29. Have you ever tested cleaning employees to determine their understanding of their job and duties?

30. Have work samplings been made to determine the time employees actually spent

in productive work?

31. Is recognition or reward given to personnel who do exceptionally good work?

32. Are rewards given for good suggestions?

33. Are written qualifications used for hiring workers?

34. Are physical examinations given to prospective employees?

35. Are cleaning workers trained before new building occupancy?

36. Do you conduct regular scheduled maintenance inspections?

37. Do you have an efficient system for stocking, keeping inventory, and distributing cleaning equipment and supplies?

38. Are custodial facilities adequate from the standpoint of size, number, location, and furnishings?

39. Do your employees feel that management is interested in their work and their problems?

40. Does your school have a continuing awareness and interdepartmental cooperation program related to housekeeping?

41. Is the custodial department consulted when plans are made for new construction?

42. Do you require your suppliers to provide demonstrations and other services?

43. Have you recently reviewed your maintenance practices from the standpoint of safety?

44. Do you regularly read current literature concerning housekeeping?

45. Is maintenance equipment cleaned after each day of use?

46. Are adequate records maintained to insure proper protection of surfaces at proper intervals (such as resealing floors)?

47. Are adequate records kept to show what supplies are used and how much of each item is required per month?

48. Are records maintained as to the nature and source of complaints concerning housekeeping?

49. Are complaints studied periodically to determine how the general situation can be improved?

50. Are regular reports made to management on progress of the cleaning program?

Unfortunately, housekeeping and maintenance facilities usually rank low on an administrator's priority list of job responsibilities. This may explain in part why so many schools across the country register relatively high maintenance costs or why so many unkempt and unattractive facilities can be found.

Maintenance is a problem that doesn't stop, then start, and then stop again. It is a continuing component of school operation that must be analyzed and planned for. The prime emphasis of a plant operation program should be to focus on preventive maintenance instead of the catch up and patch program that is normally followed. Keep in mind that the building is the largest piece of instructional equipment available. Poorly kept buildings may reduce instructional effectiveness as well as lower staff morale and community pride.

A SYSTEM

A systematic approach to the cleaning of instructional facilities is vital to learning and public relations. There is no reason why the administrator cannot devise an efficient plan of action for facility housekeeping functions.

Certain factors will influence the action system. Consideration must be given to the following: (1) How do I evaluate my program? (2) How do I train my custodial personnel? (3) What are the workloads, schedules, and job controls? (4) How do I motivate my personnel to perform their tasks efficiently? (5) What is the best way to standardize my equipment? (6) How do I involve the students and staff in developing pride in an attractive building and working in harmony with the custodial program? (7) Where do I find the research programs leading to improved custodial methods? (8) How can I introduce new materials that are highly maintenance free into the school?

A concerted effort to find the answers to the above questions as they apply to your facility is necessary to develop a quality housekeeping system.

Personnel

The major key to quality school housekeeping and maintenance, of course, is the quality of personnel responsible for executing the program. To hire and keep marginal workers means that the custodial program will never develop beyond the mop and bucket stage.

Having so many demands on the school budget dollar means that we deceive ourselves into believing that poorly paid and incompetent people can fulfill the housekeeping demands in today's complex educational facilities. Today, more than ever, school people are having to defend their budget expenditures in light of the performance of dollars spent. This leads directly to careful consideration of characteristics of personnel to be hired. When hiring of personnel is anticipated, specific duties and responsibilities of the custodial position should accompany the announcement of a vacancy on the staff. Advertising in the paper, notice to the state employment agency, and word of mouth are normal procedures for recruitment. Completion of application forms should be standard procedure for the applicants. Letters of reference should support the form. A critical review of the data on the person's background follows to include such considerations as health, emotional stability, and how a person relates with people.

Finchum[3] offered the following as desirable qualifications for those who perform custodial services:

Good health and vigor
Absence of physical defects
Average or better than average mental ability
At least an eighth grade education, but
    preferably high school
Superior character, cooperative attitude,
    sense of responsibility, neat, clean
    appearance, pleasing voice, acceptable
    language habits, proficiency in modern
    school plant operating techniques
A knowledge of the fundamentals of: school
    health and sanitation, heating-ventilation,
    plumbing, electricity, air-conditioning,
    lighting, cleaning techniques and good
    housekeeping practices
Have a respect for children
Related experience, or willingness to be
    trained
Age not under 21 nor over 45

The above, at first glance, appear to be stringent demands for employment. However, they really are minimal to carry out a custodial program that will help ensure a quality environment in the school. Another thought that appears after reading the characteristics demanded is that a man with such capabilities could command a larger salary than is usually paid custodians. This is true; however, the possibility is great that a man meeting these requirements would probably be more effective than two or three low potential custodial position applicants.

After the custodian has been employed, he should not be left to his own devices to learn the routines of the work. Self-instruction or learning by experience alone can be time consuming and costly. In-service training should be provided for custodial employees. Instructors can be administrators; however, experienced maintenance men and experienced custodians normally should carry out the training assignment. One very valuable training resource for the administrator is the use of industrial firms who are directly involved in the sales of cleaning materials and equipment. They normally take information concerning new cleaning techniques and make themselves available for custodial training sessions.

In schools with more than one custodial person, the administrator should designate one person as a head custodian or supervisor. The head custodian should be given the responsibility of assigning personnel after determining the right work load. His assignments should not be made by word of mouth but by written work schedules. The following is an example of a daily cleaning schedule.

Daily Custodian Cleaning Schedule, High School

Joe Smith - 3:30 p.m.-12:00 p.m.

   3:30 Check note box for other than
          routine cleaning or maintenance
          instructions from head custodian

or administrator. Put all
necessary cleaning and maintenance equipment on cleaning
wagon.

3:45   Pick up paper and debris on
outside assigned area.

4:10   Start cleaning assigned areas.
a. Pick up papers and other debris
on carpeted floor. Every third
day or when needed vacuum floors.
Remove spots from carpet when
needed.
b. Empty wastepaper holders and
pencil sharpeners.
c. Arrange furniture as stipulated
by teacher.
d. Dust all furniture and cabinet
surfaces with hand duster.
e. Close windows, turn off lights,
and lock doors.

6:30   Clean assigned restroom areas for
night use.

7:00   Eat dinner.

7:30   Continue room cleaning assignments.

10:15   Coffee break.

10:30   Complete room cleaning.

11:00   Sweep or vacuum assigned corridor
area.

11:30   Check restrooms for final cleaning
after night use.

11:45   Check mechanical air or heat. Make
fire and locked door check. Turn
off lights except those designated
to be left on for safety purposes.

The head custodian should focus on quality control of work and workers by a feasible rating system. He must set standards for cleaning performance and through the use of checklists ascertain the degree to which standards have been met.

Good supervision can and will cut costs and improve the standard of cleaning. The head janitor and administrator should select products and equipment that best solve their cleaning problems. Certainly the areas of work should be analyzed in terms of quality and cost. It is imperative to determine if the materials and equipment will contribute to solving the problem, hindering its solution, or raising costs beyond desired benefits.

It is not an easy task to know what the right products and equipment are. The administrator may seek guidance from industrial experts to point to problem solutions. Select two, three, or more companies to demonstrate how they would solve a cleaning problem. Apply quality and cost values to each demonstration and then make a decision. There is no reason to limit the search to the opinion of one salesman or one company. Be wary of those who seek to sell a product but offer no further service. These people are not likely to help utilize the operations budget in a way that provides a maximum benefit and return to the school for each housekeeping dollar invested.

Planning for a Custodial Program

A first step in planning for inside and outside cleaning is to collect and organize data regarding all of the areas that need to be cleaned and maintained for your building. Usually this survey can be made by the administrator with the aid of the head janitor and a district maintenance supervisor. When the survey of the building has been completed, all cleaning and maintenance needs should be tabulated to show costs, priority, and frequency of cleaning and maintenance.

From the above survey, the administrator can work out cleaning schedules with the head custodian for his staff. The survey also provides excellent information for the administrator in determining budget requests for cleaning and maintenance of his/her school. Probably not all maintenance or cleaning needs will be approved for the school's budget; however, you can defend your budget request with the survey data. List all your needs on a priority basis. If your budget request is not fulfilled, then you will know exactly what can be done with the money that has been allotted. Many times when an administrator shows a well documented need list with priorities, he/she will receive more funds than the one who asks for a stipulated amount with little backup data.

After a yearly comprehensive survey of the cleaning and maintenance needs of a building is made, the administrator should make periodic checks of the facility. Particular attention should be focused on conditions that promote safety and health for teachers and students. Be alert to potential hazards. Another valuable reason for making periodic checks of cleaning and maintenance efforts is to evaluate the quality of work maintained by the cleaning staff. The following could serve as a guide for a weekly cleaning and maintenance facility check and evaluation.

Weekly Cleaning and Maintenance Facility Checklist

Inside:

Are lights operating?
Is room equipment in good repair?
Are specified quality cleaning standards being maintained?
Do doors easily open and close?
Are door closures and door stops in good working order?
Is room furniture in good repair?
Are there any safety problems such as broken or cracked windows, frayed

electrical wire extensions, loose
lighting fixtures, bulbs, or lamps?
Do all utilities operate efficiently?
Are soap dispensers, towel dispenser,
and restroom areas well supplied
with needed materials?

Outside:

Are outside windows clean?
Are there any safety hazards?
Are there sufficient waste disposals and
are they emptied regularly?
Is outside lighting operating?
Are previously determined quality cleaning
standards being met?
Are outside wall and window areas in good
repair?
Are all landscaped areas being maintained
to standard?

Inside Cleaning and Maintenance

Inside cleaning and maintenance are services
provided to keep the facility in good condition,
safe, and functional for the educational activities
that are to be carried out in the building. Normally, cleaning and maintenance components within
the school would be furniture and equipment (fixed
or movable), thermal environment systems, lighting
systems, floors, other surfaces and finishes, doors,
and windows. The following are some guidelines for
inside cleaning and maintenance for special areas
within the school building.

Cleaning and maintaining floors involves a
crucial choice of equipment and cleaning products.
Equipment plays a great motivational role in providing greater quality coverage. Although the
initial expense may be high, stainless steel equipment has many advantages in the long run. Large
corridors are maintained more efficiently with
automated riding equipment for waxing, polishing,
cleaning, and dusting.

Evaluation of floor surfaces should be made prior to selecting the appropriate floor finish. Basically, a floor finish is a removable coating designed to minimize floor wear through scuffing and traffic wear and tear. A finish should make floor maintenance easier, as well as improve appearance.

What are some of the qualities to look for in floor finishes? They should have or provide: good appearance qualities, resistance to soil, no odor, no change in floor color, safety for users to prevent falls and slippery conditions, easy to strip and remove, no chemical reaction that would cause fire or health problems, and durability.

After selection of equipment and products for floor cleaning has been made, a set of procedures should be established for cleaning and maintenance. The old approach--spending a great deal of time in summer months to process floors--never was efficient in time or cost. The answer is to provide more frequent floor treatment throughout the school year. A number of systems are now in use for cleaning and maintaining floors. The administrator can select one to meet the school's unique cleaning and maintenance problems.

One system that holds great promise is now in use in a number of school districts where regular floor treatment is provided every six weeks. The result is cleaner floors, a 25 percent cut in upkeep costs, and a 50 percent decrease in time expenses. School Management described one such system developed by a commercial concern as follows:

"The system, which is most effective when used on wood and/or tile floors which have previously been treated with a good floor base, can be used in any school by any two custodians, using any quality cleaning and finishing liquids.

Here's how it works:

-140-

Step 1. Floor maintenance begins with the team of two custodians depositing their equipment--solutions, mop and pail, automatic floor machine--in the first classroom to be cleaned and clearing one-half the room of furniture. This is done by moving desks and chairs to the wall nearest the door. Bookcases and other heavy furniture standing against the walls are left in place on the assumption that the floor beneath is in good shape.

The two custodians immediately repeat this process in four adjacent classrooms. And, in three additional rooms, they move only the heavy teachers' desks. Then, one of them returns to the starting point and begins cleaning...while the other stays behind to move the remaining lighter furniture.

Step 2. When the last chair and desk have been moved, the second custodian returns to the starting point, where his teammate has already begun applying scrubbing solution with the mop. The second custodian follows behind with the automatic floor machine--going over the floor once with the scrubbing action, a second time to rinse.

Both men stay one tile away from the walls of the room and three tiles from the corners, since these areas are usually not worn. Skipping them cuts cleaning time.

Step 3. The first custodian continues applying scrubbing solution until he has done all eight cleared classrooms. He then returns to the starting point and begins to lay finish (i.e., wax) over the floors, which have been scrubbed, rinsed, and are dry. Meanwhile, the second custodian completes scrubbing and rinsing the remaining rooms, returns to the starting point, moves all scrubbing equipment to a new block of eight rooms and begins moving the lighter furniture in these.

Step 4. When the first custodian has finished applying finish to the floors in the first block of classrooms, he moves to the second block and he and his teammate move the <u>heavy</u> furniture in each room. The second custodian then continues moving the lighter desks and chairs while the first man goes to the cleaning equipment and once again, begins applying scrubbing solution.

Step 5. Scrubbing, rinsing, and the application of floor finish proceeds as in the first block of eight rooms (see steps 3 and 4 above) until both blocks of eight classrooms are half done. The custodians then return to the first block of eight rooms to finish the other half. This involves repeating the entire process on the unfinished sections of floor. That is:

1. Custodian 1 applies scrubbing solution to unfinished half of eight classrooms.

2. Custodian 2 moves remaining furniture in eight rooms, then returns to base room and automatic floor machine.

3. Custodian 1 completes application of scrubbing solution in eight rooms, returns to base, and begins applying finish.

4. Custodian 1 finishes work with automatic floor machine and goes

to second block of eight rooms to
move lighter furniture.

5. Custodian 1 completes application
   of finish, helps Custodian 2 move
   heavy furniture in second block of
   eight classrooms, then begins applying scrubbing solution.

6. Custodian 2 follows after with scrubbing machine.

7. Custodian 1 applies finish.

Step 6. When both blocks of eight classrooms have been completely gone over, the
maintenance team of two men returns to the
first room and begins arranging furniture
as it had been before the job was begun.
Only the heaviest finish--which dries in
a matter of two hours on the average--will
take sliding of the lighter furniture without marking.

With all furniture returned to its usual
place, the job is complete. Time elapsed?
It depends on the kinds of classrooms being
cleaned--laboratories, for example, take
longer. But a good average is 16 rooms in
a seven-hour shift."[4]

Carpeted floor care demands a much different
use of products and equipment because of the nature
of carpet material. Some research supports the
conclusion that carpeted areas in schools cost less
to maintain than non-carpeted floors.

In general, the housekeeping requirement for
carpeted floors is daily machine vacuuming. Daily
spot cleaning, where needed, can be done by providing the custodian with a small spot remover
kit. Under ordinary circumstances, the use of a
neutral detergent with water will clean most spots.
It is necessary to get to the stain quickly. The

frequency of overall cleaning with shampoo, other cleaning solutions, scrubbing machines, and wet pick-up vacuums is determined by the use of the carpeted area and the kind of soil the carpet is subjected to. Some districts completely clean carpets twice a year, others once a year, and some wait as long as two years.

Most commercial carpet cleaning firms will contract to clean carpet either in place or will remove it and clean it in their cleaning establishments. Some industrial carpet cleaners provide the carpet and its maintenance with a long-term cleaning contract established with the school district. There are a number of ways to provide for the maintenance of carpeting. The sub-contractor who laid your carpet may supply any special cleaning instructions. A local carpet jobber will work with you in preparing a good plan for cleaning and maintaining the school carpet.

Washrooms can be the source of a variety of problems. If special and continued attention is focused on washroom areas, many student problems can be eliminated. Paper drying towels and the roll-type cloth towels may generate problems. Paper towels thrown away carelessly lead to clogging of wash basins and toilets. They may litter the floor as well. Carelessly used roll-type cloth towels lead to sanitary problems if students do not roll to an unused area but merely dry hands and face on used portion of towel. Some use this as an argument for hot air dryers to replace paper and roll type cloth towels. The dryers eliminate paper problems and at the same time provide a good sanitary condition. Hot air dryers, on the other hand, are slower and may not be used by those in a hurry or with an aversion for the noisy devices.

To maintain the washroom area, it is necessary that the area be checked every two hours, at the maximum, by the custodial personnel. Under no conditions should this ever be the job of the

teaching staff. Spot checks of restroom areas may
limit the tendency to use them as smoking places
by some secondary students as well as insure cleaner
facilities.

Beginning with the correct surface (ceramic
walls and floors) can help to minimize the maintenance. Easy to clean surfaces are usually attractive as well. Cleaning the walls normally consists
of daily spot cleaning with a general washing of
walls and floors once a week. Another suggestion
for helping to provide a good washroom area is to
replace hand flushed urinals and toilets with an
automated flushing system. This will systematic-
ally eliminate major odor and debris problems that
usually exist in a hand-flushed toilet and urinal
washroom. Also, providing automatic turn off
handles on the wash basin faucets is a great aid
in reducing basin overflows. In areas where water
costs are at a premium, it certainly can be a great
water and cost saving device.

A system of cleaning washrooms must be developed so that all areas will be subjected to cleaning routine. The following is a cleaning routine
suggested by Smalley as a good basic approach to
washroom cleaning and maintenance:

"Following is a routine for the maintenance
as recommended some time ago by the National
Sanitary Supply Association: (1) Empty all
trash receptacles in a canvas truck. (2) Re-
fill the towel dispenser. (3) Fill all soap
dispensers. (4) Check the deodorant dispensers. It is to be remembered that the deodorant blocks (paradichlorbenzine) are effective
only below. The gas they liberate is said
to be five times heavier than the air and,
therefore, descends, theoretically pressing
the foul odor down. (5) Clean light fixtures.
Adequate lighting is essential to a well-
maintained washroom. (6) Use drainpipe
cleaner periodically, and use a "plumber's
friend" to force down clogging water.

-145-

(7) Keep the windows clean, not only for sanitary reasons but to increase the daytime light. (8) Spotclean the walls daily. (9) Clean the mirrors. (10) Wash the basins, using an abrasive powder cleaner. Rinse and wipe dry. (11) Sanitize the toilet seat, using a cellulose sponge dipped in disinfecting solution. Clean both top and bottom of the seat. The bowl should also be cleaned each day with a good bowl cleaner and bowl brush, being careful to clean, as much as possible, the groove under the top of the bowl. (12) Mop the floor daily, using an antiseptic cleaner in the mop water."[5]

We have discussed a few solutions to school cleaning problems. Most facility cleaning problems can be solved by the administrator, his/her cleaning consultants, and staff if time is taken to analyze what must be done, when, how, and by whom. The point is that the administrator as a manager of the facility that houses learners and teachers must develop the expertise to insure that the building is safe, clean, and an attractive learning environment.

TEACHER-STUDENT-CUSTODIAN RELATIONSHIP

It is essential that students and faculty understand the role of the custodian in your school. Students and teachers must feel they are part of the learning environment and have a responsibility in keeping the building safe, clean, and attractive. Teachers should be given this responsibility of seeing that their teaching and learning areas are free of unnecessary debris thrown carelessly by students. It will normally take a minute or two of the class time for students to clean up floor, desk, table, and special areas. It is a simple contribution to ecology and fosters good citizenship habits.

Your plant operation policy should direct students and teachers to be responsible for cleaning their areas at the end of each class period for two major reasons:

1. The concept of being responsible for an orderly appearance in the school facility should carry over to the home and other areas of the community. If the school does not accept the responsibility for developing this concept, then it is failing to provide a basic approach to life in our society. This is more important than ever at a time when everyone is being recruited in the battle against polution of the environment.

2. With a little help from everyone in the school situation, the cleaning problem can be reduced to a point where the custodians can focus their effort on the cleaning functions that demand special equipment and cleaning materials. A more efficient use of the custodian's time can provide for a cleaner facility.

Over the years, there has been some friction between custodians and teachers who move the room furniture into a variety of seating and work arrangements. The teacher should be encouraged in every way to utilize equipment and furniture in the way that best suits his/her needs for classroom learning situations. Under no circumstances should the custodian dictate how learning equipment should be arranged or utilized by a teacher or pupil. The custodian is charged with cleaning the teaching space and returning the furniture to the positions the teacher feels is best for learning.

Another trouble spot for teacher-custodian relationship over the years has been the decorating of a space for certain special occasions that take place each year, such as: Halloween, Thanksgiving,

Christmas, etc. There is no one way to approach this problem. Again, the school exists for the learner and not for the convenience of the custodians. Normally it is the responsibility of the teacher and the students to decorate for an occasion without destroying walls and other surfaces. They may remove the special decorations for future use. Teachers and students should be advised and realize that when they are developing decorative plans, consideration should be given to clean-up after the event.

Within each school, a custodian should be given the responsibility of bringing to the attention of the administrator, or head custodian, depending upon the size of the school, those students and teachers who are responsible for excessive cleaning problems. There is no reason why a cooperative and effective plan of action cannot be developed to expedite a facility cleaning program that is beneficial to student, teacher, custodian, administrator, and community. The appearance and operating costs of a hundred thousand to a multi-million dollar school facility is greatly influenced by how well the administrator discharges this responsibility.

SUMMARY

Facility pupil capacity can be determined in a variety of ways. The educational program should and must have the greatest influence upon the extent of pupil capacity. When facilities become over-crowded, it almost immediately reduces educational opportunities for students. There are usually three measures that are evaluated to determine the usefulness of a school. They are: (1) rated pupil capacity for a given educational program; (2) an index of educational adequacy based on the number and design of educational spaces necessary to facilitate a desirable curriculum for students of elementary or secondary school age; and (3) the physical condition of the structure, the site, and service systems. It is almost impossible to examine an empty facility and arrive at pupil capacity. The same plant could have very different rated capacities for two different educational programs.

Without doubt the number of instructional periods or units will have a direct effect on the pupil capacity of a school. An eight or nine period school day increases the probability for number of students served over a five or six period day. Many schools with space problems have had to increase the number of periods per day to accommodate increasing enrollments. The complicated structure and organization of our elementary and secondary school buildings defy developing a rigid rule for determining the pupil capacity of school buildings.

An attractive and well kept facility must be planned. A quality operation and maintenance program for the facility is important for students and teachers primarily for health and safety reasons. The major key to quality school housekeeping and maintenance is the quality of personnel responsible for executing the program. A daily schedule for cleaning must be established. Good supervision can and will cut costs and improve the standard of cleaning. Planning for inside and outside cleaning is a must. Data must be collected and organized regarding all areas that need to be cleaned and maintained. A survey can help in establishing cleaning budget needs and the development of a daily cleaning schedule.

The administrator and the head custodian must identify cleaning problems and work out the solutions to those problems. Most facility cleaning problems can be solved by the administrator, his/her cleaning consultants from the central office or industry, and his/her staff, both professional and classified. It is essential that teachers and students understand the role of the custodian. Each should support the work of the custodian. On the other hand, the custodian should understand that he is there to support the work of faculty and students and that a cooperative effort must be made by all to provide a clean and well kept facility.

NOTES

1. S.J. Knezevich, "A Procrustean Bed or Functional School Plant," <u>American School Board Journal</u> (November, 1971). Used by permission.

2. Edwin E. Feldman, "How to Get Your Maintenance Program Organized," <u>School Management</u> (May, 1965): pp. 95-96.

3. R.N. Finchum, "Administering the Custodial Program," <u>School Plant Management Bulletin</u>, (Washington, D.C.). Used by permission.

4. West Coast Representative of the Acme Chemical Company, "How to Clean Your Floors Faster--Cheaper--Better," <u>School Management</u> (December, 1966): pp. 57-58.

5. Dave E. Smalley, "The Care of Washrooms," <u>The American School Board Journal</u> (September, 1964): p. 41. Used by permission.

CHAPTER V

CHALLENGES FOR THE ADMINISTRATOR

The administrator cannot escape responsibility for what goes on in the building. He must have a strategy and plan of action for plant safety and public use activities.

SCHOOL SAFETY

So often we are caught up in trying to solve a safety problem after an accident or near miss. A prevention program of safety is a realistic part of a well managed school. It is clearly evident that a very high percentage of school accidents could have been prevented. Teachers, students, non-teaching staff, and administrators have to be aware of potential dangers. The following are typical measures for the administrator to note when establishing safety procedures for his/her faculty.

Overloading hallways with students is a common practice and it provides a natural way to jostle and be jostled. Student traffic patterns should be analyzed. If there is too great a con-centration of students in one area at a certain time, then they should be re-routed.

Girls' and boys' physical education areas provide many safety hazards. Soap outlets or containers should be checked to prevent the soap from leaking on the shower floor causing a very slick and slippery surface. A student drying area should be established next to the shower entrance with some type of rough surface to reduce the possibilities of slipping and falling. Many physical education areas are designed so that towel dispensing centers are across the room from shower exits. Towels should be given to students as soon as they leave the shower area. Many older schools have broken tile on shower walls and broken tile on shower floors. These result in many minor painful cuts on hands, fingers, and toes.

Every school comes under some type of legal requirements concerning what to do in case of fire. Often the fire drill is considered a farce by teachers and students alike. A good policy is one which directs staff to take one minute every so often to discuss quickly but surely the directions for leaving the building under disaster or fire conditions. Fire departments will cooperate in many ways to provide the kind of help needed to develop attitudes for fire prevention. Having the fire department supervise your fire drills and give a written critique of the drill to be printed in the school newspaper or daily bulletin is a good idea. Praising good fire drill practices of certain rooms or grades can lead to competitive action throughout the student body.

Another task where the fire department can be of great help is that of inspecting the facility from time to time for fire hazards. Some teachers and some administrators are notorious for keeping everything that has ever come into their possession. After a short while closets are filled with unusable, but highly inflammable, materials. Boxes of junk are stored in basements or in attics. Storage areas under stairwells in older buildings are filled with combustible materials. Firemen are trained to recognize fire safety problems and should be used for that purpose. The administrator should utilize their services frequently to protect his or her students and facility from the ever-present danger of fire.

An effective program of safety starts with the administrator and his/her staff. Some areas of the building are more prone to accidents than others because of activities or materials that are a basic part of that environment. The areas of industrial arts, general science, vocational-technical shops, ceramic art rooms, chemistry labs, home economic sewing and cooking, physical education, and photo darkrooms all have greater potential for accidents than other classroom areas. Staff members in the above mentioned areas must have safety concepts built into their teaching activities.

Some administrators allow teachers to leave their areas without supervision. In fact, teachers have been called out of their teaching space by the administrator to attend to some administrative detail and students have been hurt because of lack of supervision at that moment. It is the responsibility of the administrator to request from his or her staff members the procedures of safety that are utilized in the accident prone areas.

Newer schools have many built-in safety devices. Older schools should be brought up to date by installing modern safety devices. An example would be to provide a master electric switch in each shop area. A teacher looking at his students at their working stations could detect a very dangerous situation and prevent an accident by cutting off the power. When purchasing equipment for any area of the school, find out the safety features of that particular design and model.

Bicycle safety programs are essential for elementary and junior high schools. The placing of bicycle storage racks at points on the campus that do not conflict with automobile transportation is very important. Many times bicycle storage is placed next to teacher and visitor parking areas. This creates a very accident-prone situation in which cars and bicycles may tangle. Police departments throughout the country will aid in developing and carrying out a bicycle safety program. A day or two after school opens in the fall is an excellent time to have an outside bicycle safety assembly. Students need to be reinforced after their long summer vacation season concerning good bicycle procedure at school and on the city streets.

For high school students, one of the greatest accident prevention programs is the satisfactory completion of a driver education class. There is overwhelming evidence that driver education class students are much less accident-prone than students who have learned to drive from different sources. A high school principal should try in every way possible to have this included as an intricate part of the school program.

Student automobiles on the high school campus always provide some danger potential. Some principals establish that if a student brings a car onto a campus, it must not be moved until the student goes home in the afternoon. This is well and good for the student who brings his car to school and parks it in the school parking area. But what of the students who do not want to abide by the school parking rule and choose to park off-campus? This many times provides a nuisance factor for the school neighbors who have cars parked in front of their residences all day.

School parking areas can be improved so that hazards are reduced. Areas should be well marked. Spaces for parking should be wide enough to allow safe parking without having to inch by a parked car. Entrance and exit areas should be at opposite ends of the parking areas. Slow speed rates should be enforced. Parking spaces should be arranged so that students do not have to walk behind cars to get to their own.

Students who drive cars to school should be provided with some kind of an identifying emblem or sticker. They should receive the emblem or sticker after attending and participating in a school parking accident prevention session. The session should be designed around the safety factors that should be observed for on-campus parking. Students should also be encouraged to discuss and recommend changes in established parking regulations that are not providing an efficient approach to automobile movement on campus. The parking accident prevention session should be interesting, helpful, and not long. Using students as driver demonstrators is a good method to keep other students interested in what is being said and done. Choose other students at random to demonstrate how they would enter the parking lot or leave or park their car. This is another occasion when the police, state vehicle department personnel, and city and county safety personnel can be of great aid in developing and carrying out the program.

Safety conscious behavior just doesn't happen. Like anything else there must be an organized plan designed and put into action to yield the desired behavior. Students, teachers, and administrators must establish written policy on safety procedures to be followed in classroom and facility situations. The major premise of the safety program should be to provide an accident-free education to the extent that the facility and human nature will permit.

The administrator has the responsibility of setting the direction of the safety program. His or her initiative and knowledge of safety procedures determine the effectiveness of the program. Kigin[1] provides the following guidelines for the development of a school safety program:

1. Identify and select an advisory committee with representation from the pupils, the administration, and all academic disciplines.

2. Develop a safety manual for the school.

3. Develop a standard accident reporting form.

4. Develop a standard procedure to follow in the event of an accident.

5. Control class size in keeping with sound educational practices and the ability of teachers to supervise.

6. Standardize fire extinguishers in all classrooms, shops, and laboratories.

7. Utilize posters and other visual aids to constantly remind pupils of proper safety practices.

8. Clearly post emergency procedures, such as instructions for exiting the building in case of fire.

9. Investigate the possibility of a 100 percent eye safety program in all activity laboratories.

10. Encourage all teachers, administrators, and noninstructional staff to set the best possible example of safety for the pupils.

MANAGEMENT OF AFTER-SCHOOL FACILITY USE

The after-school use of facilities has been a problem for years and is even a greater one today. Most of the time the after-school use policy is spelled out for the administrator by the school board. The policy may be weak and ineffective. Administrators are asked from time to time for ideas and recommendations to improve the after-school facility use policy. Several factors must be considered. Unless the school board or superintendent has policies to the contrary, the administrator is responsible for building utilization after as well as during school hours.

One of the first questions raised when discussing after school facility use is what fee shall be charged. Generally school and school related groups should not pay fees or rental charges for the use of the facilities for school or school related purposes. The use of extra equipment or a heavy use of custodial or maintenance personnel might sometimes require a small fee. It should be remembered that the facility was constructed to provide learning activities for people of all ages.

All non-school groups should pay some kind of fee for facility use. The charges should be based on the cost of utilities and the cost of custodial and supervisory personnel needed for a particular occasion. Actual labor costs and estimated hourly utility costs should determine the fee. Profit is not the motive and should not be anticipated. By the same token, usage not related to educational purposes should not be allowed to be a drain on school dollars that are best dedicated to enhancing learning.

The school should not be in the business of renting its facilities. Competition with other facility resources in a community does not make for good public relations. Holding non-school group dances, dinners, movies, and other activities that compete with local merchants is usually a poor use of the facility. However, if activities as stated above are not offered by private businessmen, then the school can be utilized to function as a community center for those activities. If food is handled and sold in the school to non-school groups, it should be sponsored by the school and profits should be placed in the student body fund or be stipulated for a particular school group that worked on the preparation and serving of food. It is just not wise, in most instances, to allow an outside the school non-related school group to use the school facility for profit.

Many schools have lighting equipment, recording equipment or expensive equipment of one kind or another. School-connected personnel should be required to operate the equipment and be paid for their time. The school should not have to suffer the consequences of expensive repair and non-use inconvenience during repair which are the result of allowing inexperienced operators to use school equipment. Many times policemen and firemen are needed to protect school facilities. Their time should be paid for by the non-school group using the facility.

What are some general facility restrictions that are usually enforced for group use? A list of restrictions described in a study of after-school use policies of nine major school districts by Finchum are:

> School facilities cannot be used by an individual, group, or organization for any activity that is intended to over-throw the government by force, violence, or other unlawful means.

> Games of chance, lotteries, or other acti-vities classified as gambling cannot be conducted on school premises.

> Alcoholic beverages, tobacco, or other products considered hazards to health cannot be sold on school premises.

> No enterprise, function, or activity that promotes any commercial product or results in private profit or commercial gain for any business enterprise can be conducted on school property.

> Activities in conflict with city ordinances or state laws are not permitted.

> Smoking is prohibited on school premises except under prescribed conditions.[2]

The above restrictions would be useful in most policy statements. There are local mores, beliefs, and customs that will dictate other restrictions for school use and these should be taken into con-sideration when developing policy.

A written application form and a written contract agreement should be required from all non-school related groups who desire to use the building. The school and school district need these forms to plan and carry out an efficient after-school facility use program. Application forms and contracts should be developed within the statute requirements of the political sub-division that has legal jurisdiction over the school. The district attorney, county counsel, city attorney, or whoever is utilized as a legal authority of the board should be consulted con-cerning the design of the document. One appli-cation facility use form or contract form cannot be offered at present as a standard for all schools or school districts because of nationwide conflict-ing laws and opinions concerning facility use.

The sample forms given in Figures 2 and 3 could be used as guides for developing forms for your school's after-school facility use policy. One is a sample application form to be submitted to the school, and the other is a sample contract for facility use.

It is good management to require insurance coverage on the part of the user. The user's insurance agent should deliver a statement to you before the facility is used stating that agreed insurance bond amount is in force. The school cannot risk having to pay for damage or personal injury caused by non-related group use of the school facility.

Some districts demand a rental fee payment before use. The best policy is to establish a reasonable time for payment after the group has used the facility. Be sure that the school dis-trict's legal counsel approves the contractual form before you sign or ask the user to sign the agreement.

One major policy factor that should be fol-lowed is to have a reliable administrator or staff members supervise each after-school use facility function. It is imperative that a person closely

FIGURE 2.

Application for the Use of School Facilities
by Non-School Groups

Applicant (Name of Group):   Date:
Address: Phone:

Name of Person Responsible for School Use:
Address: Phone:

State specific space or spaces required for function:

Describe activities for planned event:

Requested date and time:

Open facility at:

Close facility at:

What school equipment will be required?

APPROVAL:

Principal_____   Date:

School District_____   Date:

(Approval by a school district official is a good
backup for the principal. There will be times when
the policy will not permit the approval of an application and two levels of disapproval will usually
eliminate some problems. Another reason for district approval is to coordinate the district use
of school facilities.)

-162-

FIGURE 3.

(School District Name)

The _____ has requested the use of
          organization or person

_____ for a
   name of school and specific space or spaces

meeting on _____ at _____.

    The person responsible for the function is:

Name:

Address: Phone:

It is understood that the above organization will be responsible for personal liabilities and property damages to the
school or persons using the facilities while under its
direction.

The rental fee will be $_____ to include utility
costs and the following personnel:

It is agreed that the user will furnish a liability insurance
bond for $_____. This bond will cover possible per-
sonal injury or repair of damage to the facility by the user.
The user agrees to pay the rental fee to the (name of school
district) within a three-day period after the function.

_____   _____
   Applicant Signature   School District Signature

associated with the school be there to make decisions about facility use so that accidents, damage
to equipment, furniture, and the facility can be
kept to a bare minimum. Non-school related groups
in most cases should be charged for school staff
supervision and it should be part of the overall
fee.

After-school use of the facility by non-school
related groups can be a public relations boon or
a headache. Community groups should be able to
utilize school facilities for acceptable activities.
School-community relations can be greatly enhanced
when a workable after-school use facility policy is
developed and put into practice.

SUMMARY

Safety procedures and public use of the school
facility have for many years been problem areas for
the school administrator.

School safety problems can be solved best by
anticipating what the problems are and taking care
of them before an accident or near miss occurs.
Each school will have particular safety problems.
Over-loaded hallways, girls' and boys' physical
education, and stair areas are major hazard spots
within the school. School administrators can receive help in identifying safety hazards by asking
for help from local fire, police, and insurance
people.

A safety conscious behavior on the part of
staff and students must be the result of an organized plan to provide an accident-free education.
The administrator has the responsibility of setting
the direction of the safety program. Teachers and
students should be indoctrinated and oriented concerning safety behavior. The physical plant must
be continually checked by custodial staff for
dangers that might develop that could injure school
personnel.

The school should not be in the business of renting its facilities. It should not compete with other facility resources within the community for renting purposes. Those non-school groups who need meeting space and can go only to the school should pay some kind of fee for facility use. The charge should be based upon cost of utilities and the cost of custodial and supervisory personnel required for the occasion. Profit should never be the motive. A policy statement should be written concerning after-hour use of the school facility by non-school related groups. Written application facility use forms and written agreement forms should be developed and used for the school's protection. Community groups should be able to utilize school facilities for acceptable activities, but a workable after-school use facility policy must be developed and closely adhered to.

NOTES

1. Dennis Kigin, "Compare School Programs to Established Criteria," <u>The American School Board Journal</u> (July, 1967): pp. 13-16. Used by permission.

2. R.N. Finchum, <u>Extended Use of School Facilities</u> (Washington, D.C.: U.S. Department of Health, Education and Welfare, Office of Education Publication OE-21035, 1967): p. 8.

CHAPTER VI

DEALING WITH SCHOOL VANDALISM

According to Greek mythology, a certain king of Corinth was the craftiest of all men. By devious means he managed to escape death for many years, but eventually was condemned to the underworld where he was made to roll a heavy stone up a very steep hill. Every time the exhausted king approached the hilltop with his stone, it rolled back down and he was required to begin all over gain.

Combating school vandalism is in many respects analogous to the task of this legendary King Sisyphus. The work is both degrading and arduous, one's efforts are largely unavailing, any accomplishments are quite temporary, and the task extends into the future without end.

In an attempt to find answers to this seemingly intractable problem, a study has been made of British as well as American schools. The preliminary research was conducted at The Institute of Education, University of London. A survey was then made of the headteacher, ten instructors, and ten students (the latter groups randomly selected) in each of seventeen secondary schools in England and Wales. This research focused on the following four basic areas:

1. Identification of the vandals;

2. Measurement of the damage;

3. Explanations for the offensive actions; and

4. Attempts to solve the problem.

IDENTIFICATION OF THE VANDALS

In order to determine who the vandals are one must first define "vandalism." The word has reference to a Germanic people who in the 5th century A.D. ravaged Gaul and Spain, then settled in Africa and in 455 sacked Rome. It originally denoted large-scale pillaging, or robbing with open violence, but through the years its meaning has been expanded to include any act of a person willfully destroying, defacing, stealing, or setting fire to property belonging to another. And so today the term indicates a barbaric act having a senseless, ignorant, and often malicious nature.

Consider the following excerpt from the May 29, 1979, San Diego Union newspaper:

> "In March $150,000 in damage was caused by a fire in a counselor's building at O'Farrell Junior High School. Investigators termed the fire as arson and took a juvenile into custody....
>
> Most problems on school campuses and in classrooms here are caused by students, not outsiders or loiterers....
>
> Vandalism, the most common crime against school equipment and buildings, carries a national price tag of $600,000,000 annually--including the $434,522 paid last year by San Diego taxpayers."

Also reflect on the paraphrased observations of Steve Levine, a 17-year-old Denver, Colorado, student concerning the educational conditions which bring on the problem:

> "The essential nature of the public school in this country is so gloomy that it asks for destruction. Whether old or new, its floors most often are tiled, its halls usually painted tan, gray, or light green.

Its walls may be lined with that coldly
evil ceramic brick, and its cafeteria
frequently bears an odor commensurate
with the quality of the government sur-
plus food which it serves. Its classrooms are arranged as tightly as a base-
ball diamond--with one large desk facing
35 or more small ones. And as the new
'protective measures' are introduced, the
school begins to appear, and to function,
more and more like an early industrial
revolution factory.

In such an atmosphere a deeply alienated
student, a student with failing grades,
a student with poor disciplinary record,
a student who is bored, or angry, or
vindictive, a student who is unpopular
or inarticulate or frustrated, a student
with great ambitions or with no ambition
at all, has little room to breathe and
only the dimmest window out of which to
see.

He cannot effectively change the school
where he has been assigned and if he
leaves it this will jeopardize his future.
So he resorts to vandalism, whether it be
as large an act as arson or as small as
the casual dismantling of a typewriter
(a kind of activity carried out absent-
mindedly even by good students), which
offers him an avenue of expression. Such
destructive action gives him a way to
forcibly stop the educational machine--
at least temporarily. It demonstrates
his hurt and fury, and most of all, his
aching loneliness and estrangement that
are far too deep to be expunged by quick,
superficial means."

Recognizing the problem, the 92nd United
States Congress appointed a Senate Subcommittee
to investigate juvenile delinquency in the schools.

That group conducted hearings on school violence and vandalism for more than three years, and culminated their efforts with a two-volume publication containing views of the situation and possible solutions. Their findings, based on testimony of teachers, principals, students, parents, and school security officers, included the alarming conclusion that students and teachers were "becoming more concerned about self-preservation than education."

Following up on these reports, the Congress pursued the inquiry by instructing The National Institute of Education to conduct a nationwide investigation dealing in part with the school vandalism dilemma. The outcome was a three-phase study which comprised a mail survey of 4,000 elementary and secondary school principals; on-site surveys of a nationally representative cluster of 642 junior and senior high schools; and intensive qualitative case studies of ten schools. The results of this research have been compiled in a publication called Violent Schools-Safe Schools.

These reports, as well as many other treatises on the topic, list the common characteristics of school vandals. Such lists typically conclude that:

1. Vandals are most likely to be male. While research workers in both America and Britain have generally chosen to omit females in their studies, an old aphorism advises us, "If you want to know what a school is really like, go take a look at the girls' lavatories."

2. A large proportion of the vandalism is perpetrated by adolescents. Our most recent FBI Uniform Crime Reports, for example, stated that 75 percent of the persons arrested for vandalism are children under 18 years of age. Other studies have reported the modal, or most popular age for vandals to be 11 to 12 years.

3. The culprits who do the damage usually attend the victimized school. While some drop-outs and a few older persons may vandalize, most often it's the insiders, or current students, who do the "dirty work."

4. The students committing significant acts of vandalism are few in number. Studies report that less than five percent of the student body in a typical school inflict any costly damage.

5. The vandals wreak a large share of their destruction after school hours--in the evening (usually after dark) and on weekends or holidays.

6. Vandalism is primarily a group offense. It is most often committed by a band or clique of youngsters who sometimes have formed a "gang," rather than by an individual student apart from his peers.

7. Recent reports have shown that vandals also commit other criminal acts. This finding is significant because it is contrary to the findings of earlier research.

8. Most vandals have Caucasian parents who, surprisingly, are apt to be less mobile than the parents of delinquents who commit crimes other than vandalism.

9. Vandals' acts often are "out of character" considering past behavior patterns. Under certain circumstances, for example, a young, well-mannered child will try to effect the one big coup by setting fire to the school building.

10. Vandals tend to live in close proximity to the schools in which their destructive

acts occur. The building is conveniently located and unsupervised, so it is not difficult for them to break in and cause whatever damage they choose.

11. Some of the vandals have serious mental disturbances. In an isolated instance of extreme violence or destruction such as arson, the offender may be psychotic.*

While the above descriptions provide a general profile of those individuals who vandalize our schools today, the meaning of such profile could be enhanced by a delineation of the context in which they operate. Many attempts have been made to describe the schools in which the vandals cause damage, and among the findings is substantiation that:

1. The physical appearance and age of a building can have an influence on the rate of vandalism; an improved physical appearance may actually help to curb property damage.

2. More losses are incurred in schools which provide obsolete facilities and equipment.

3. Vandalism is a problem which plagues both urban and rural schools as well. The old idea that only large city schools are victimized has been largely discredited.

4. Where school administration is highly authoritarian, high property destruction costs exist.

---

* A psychotic has been defined as "a person who thinks that two plus two equals five," whereas a neurotic ' knows that two plus two equals four, but is unhappy about it."

5. In schools with low staff morale, and in those having high dissatisfaction and boredom among students, much vandalism occurs.

6. Many studies have shown that vandalism, contrary to popular belief, does not take place just in economically deprived areas. While the kinds of destructive act may differ in various locations, affluent schools as well as poor schools are subject to vandalism problems.

7. Focusing on size of schools, research indicates that vandals do more damage in large than in small schools. In this regard, a headmaster has expressed the opinion that "a school should be of such size that every teacher can be acquainted with every student, perhaps not actually being able to call his name, but knowing something about him--that he belongs in a certain room, is taking a particular course of study, or the like."

8. Integrated schools suffer less damage when they employ a high percentage of black teachers and staff members.

9. Schools with attendance problems are more troubled by vandalism than those with high average daily attendance.

10. Schools with high student-teacher ratios, and consequently large classes, are plagued with more property destruction than schools with low student-teacher ratios. While class size has not been found to be a determinant of school achievement, recent research studies have shown a positive relationship between class size and school vandalism.

Writers have attempted to describe, categorize, and classify various sorts of property destruction. They have compared instrumental vandalism to acquisitive types of vandalism, under which have been subsumed collecting vandalism, looting vandalism, and junking vandalism (in which scrap or salvage is acquired for selling to a junk dealer). Other terms that they have used to help pinpoint the destructive acts include idle, play, ignorant, clumsy, and greedy vandalism, as well as the more esoteric retributional, intentional, tactical, vindictive, and non-malicious. The category of symbolic vandalism has been divided into ideological, when the vandalism relates to a cause, and political, when it pertains specifically to government, politicians, or party activities. Examples are provided by symbolic writings on the building walls in ancient Pompeii. Some of the inscriptions recommended candidates for public office; other scratches advertised merchandise for sale; while still others were expressions of individual impulse or feeling, frequently amatory. The latter were conveyed in rude and imperfect verse, and constituted our first graffiti. More modern examples of symbolic vandalism are too commonplace to be noteworthy.

The above profile of vandals, delineation of the victimized schools, and compilation of descriptive words derive from British as well as American studies. It is interesting to note that even the stereotypes of a school vandal bear a close resemblance in the two countries. The British stereotype is of a teenage football (our soccer) hooligan, who most likely is a working class boy attending a down-town secondary modern school. As in the United States, that stereotype is not consistent with the findings in research studies. Self-report studies in England, for example, have shown that the vandal is just as likely to be a member of the middle class, and add that 85 percent of all students admit to doing things such as scratching on a desk at school, while 62 percent have been guilty of writing on walls, smashing bottles, and breaking windows. These studies also indicate that the wealthy independent schools, in which most students are middle or upper class, are no less troubled with vandalism than are state schools. The finding that vandalism is not restricted to certain social classes in England is particularly interesting in light of the greater class consciousness in that country.

The age of British vandals is generally the same as in the United States, although some studies have reported English children as young as five and six breaking into schools and causing serious property damage. Vandalism in England, as here, is a group activity often complicated by gang loyalties and rivalries, and is committed largely by youths 12 to 18 years of age. It appears that the compulsory school ages, from 5 through 16, encompass those years when students are most likely to inflict property damage. By the time they reach age 20, most young people have ceased vandalizing, but even when they have outgrown the problem, they leave behind them schools which have been scarred by their actions, and taxpayers who must pay a price to recover from the effects of their destruction.

MEASURING THE COSTS OF SCHOOL VANDALISM

Vandalism in America's schools has become a major financial consideration. During the 1960's the amount of such property destruction increased so alarmingly that Stanford Research Institute conducted a study of the situation. In the report of their findings, which they chose to call School Vandalism: A National Dilemma, the researchers estimated our nationwide damage at 200 million dollars for the 1968-69 school year. Subsequent approximations from other sources have set the figure at 400 million dollars for 1971-72 and as high as 600 million dollars for 1974-75.[1]

All reports concerning expenditures for school vandalism are only sketchy. Very few school districts collect any statistics, partly due to the many difficulties involved in determining what is

and what is not vandalism. Incidents considered
"serious" in some small schools, for example, are
often not even deemed worthy of reporting in larger
ones. Another prevalent obstacle is the fact that
school administrators are loath to admit the problem
and face up to keeping records. Even if the losses
deriving directly from vandalism could be accurately
computed, the ultimate price would still be unknown,
since so many of the costs are obscured. It is
likely, for instance, that a recently reported decline in the costs of vandalism has been more than
offset by increases in the amounts paid for security,
repairs, and insurance. The largest hidden costs
are in categories in which labor is a factor; if
the work is performed by salaried personnel, then
its costs are most likely included in operating
expenses.

The present-day 600 million dollar estimate of
annual expenditure, noted above, is an amount equi-
valent to what we spend for textbooks in the United
States; if it were possible to eliminate that expenditure, we could employ an additional 50,000
teachers with the money. Yet only a fraction of
the destructive acts are ever reported, and still
fewer of them investigated. Liability for damage
is rarely established even in the few cases where
the vandals have been identified and guilt determined.

According to one estimate based on research
conducted in the Manchester area of England, only
three percent of the vandalism cases are likely to
find their way into the records. Of course all
cases require investigation to determine whether
the damage was caused willfully, accidentally, or
if it was just the result of normal deterioration
plus "wear and tear." These things are difficult
to differentiate, and their complexity tends to
deter recordkeeping.

A large percentage of the vandalism committed
in the schools is never reported to any outside
agency or the public. In America it is customary
not to notify the police where the damage amounts

to less than 100 dollars, and not to prosecute
children who are under the age of ten. Another
important reason for the failure to report vandalism
is that many school administrators choose to hush
up or "play down" the damage, to treat it as sensitive material or information in the belief that any
news of the event will lead to publicity which will
have a detrimental effect not only in the community
but on students and staff as well. This failure to
report vandalism results, then, not only in a scar-
city of reliable statistics, but also in the lack
of opportunity for any outside agency to become
involved in solving the problem.

In England a legal framework for prosecution
is provided. There the law presumes that children
under ten years old are not aware of the meaning
of a criminal act and consequently not liable to
criminal prosecution; that children ten to fourteen
are generally incapable of committing a crime and
consequently cannot be convicted unless a court is
satisfied (a) that the child committed such act;
(b) that he or she knew that what was being done
was wrong; and (c) that he or she appreciated the
natural consequences of the act. From the age of
14 on, children are presumed capable of distin-
guishing good from evil, and must therefore accept
full responsibility for their criminal acts.

When the public thinks about school vandalism,
what immediately comes to mind is the "one big
act." This is so because the American and British
media give extensive coverage to an event such as
the intentional burning down of a school building.
It is likely, however, that the less spectacular
and more mundane acts of vandalism, such as carving
initials on desks, sticking chewing gum under chairs,
and scrawling graffiti on walls, are as costly in
the long run as the more visible and highly-publi-
cized events.

The most frequently reported act of vandalism
is window breakage. One British secondary school
sustained 140 shattered panes during the first two

weeks of a recent school year. But, as much as
the children may "love to hear the tinkle of
broken glass," still the most costly destructive
act is fire or arson. A child may set fire to a
school library, as in New Jersey recently, and
inflict 400 thousand dollars damage in a matter
of minutes. Acts of vandalism costing smaller
amounts include stealing and pilfering from schools,
scratching names and slogans on building walls,
breaking in and wrecking schoolrooms, plugging
locks with epoxy or other glue, applying spray
paint indiscriminately, breaking glass bottles on
parking lots, mutilating restroom and other walls,
stopping up sinks and turning on the water, tearing
down outside drain pipes, kicking in hallway walls,
destroying paper, supplies, records, and books,
hammering so as to dent lockers, tearing down
fences, damaging typewriters, calculators, and
duplicating machines, and initiating bomb threats.
The list is endless.

When The Working Party of The Hampshire Education Authority, England, issued a report expressing
concern about the incidence of vandalism on school
premises (1979), they singled out the most vulnerable targets for damage: windows, walls, lavatory
fittings, desks, and other furniture. The British
poet Hilaire Belloc, in his New Cautionary Tales
(1930), described the temptation this way:

> John Vavasour de Quentin Jones
> Was very fond of throwing stones
> At horses, people, passing trains,
> And especially at window panes.
> Like many of the upper class
> He liked the sound of broken glass.
> It bucked him up and made him gay,
> It was his favorite form of play.

Vandalism is not a problem peculiar to the
United States and Britain. Public discussion in
the Soviet Union, in Hungary, and elsewhere in
central Europe suggests that the phenomenon exists
there too;[2] that its causes, insofar as they can
be identified, are much the same as here; and that,

despite the application of remedies often advocated in our part of the world (strict policing, harsh sentences, community and parental responsibility, making good the damage quickly, etc.), they are nowhere near the solution. The advertisement in Figure 4 issues an appeal for help with the problem in West Germany.

Available information about the amount of school vandalism in Britain is both contradictory and confusing. On the one hand, students, teachers, and headteachers report only "a little" or "some" property damage. One headmaster put it this way: "When it's considered that we have such a small amount of supervision it is remarkable how little vandalism we suffer. Teachers' unions insist that during the lunch break no staff can be compelled to stay on duty. Some volunteers act in this way, but often the whole building and our 1,000 pupils are supervised by six or less staff."

On the other hand, research studies show large estimates of damage. The Tyne and Wear County Research Intelligence Unit estimated 1974-75 damage for the Northumbria Police Authority to be "in the range of Ł346,000 to Ł3,000,000." The Bedfordshire school authorities recently requested all schools to record incidents of damage for a four-month period and had 216 incidents reported. The Northern Ireland Education and Library Boards, surveying all post-primary and a sampling of secondary schools in 1976, estimated the annual cost of "inside" vandalism to be in excess of Ł200,000.

Colin Ward is the author of Vandalism (1975), the seminal work on the subject, and British School Buildings (1976). Noting the escalation of building costs during the 1960's and 1970's, he has reported that fire damage to school buildings rose from Ł3,000,000 in 1972 to nearly Ł9,000,000 in 1974. Pointing out that arson was involved in 398 of the 1,230 school fires recorded in 1973, he has expressed much concern about the large amount of wanton destruction in British educational buildings.

FIGURE 4.

TRANSLATION (<u>Die Welt</u>, 8/16/79)

OHNE PLATZ ZUM SPIELEN WIRD JEDES KIND BEHINDERT. ZWANGSLÄUFIG.

Wenn ein Kind aus der Monotonie
von Wohngettos nicht ausbrechen kann,
wird es anderswo aus Langeweile
einbrechen.

TATSACHE ist – Jugendkriminalität
ist da am höchsten, wo Kinder keinen
Spielraum haben.

**HELFEN SIE HEUTE,
DAMIT ES MORGEN SCHÖNER WIRD.
FÜR DIE KINDER. FÜR UNS ALLE.**

Unterstützen Sie die Arbeit des
KINDERHILFSWERKS e.V. durch einen jähr-
lichen Förderungsbeitrag von DM 24,–
oder durch eine Spende nach Ihrem
Ermessen auf das Postscheckkonto
München Nr. 440-809, BLZ 700 100 80.
KINDERHILFSWERK e.V. Langwieder
Hauptstraße 4, 8000 München 60,
Tel. 089/8 14 25 50 + 8 14 10 59.

UNSERE ZIELSÄTZE – NEUE SPIELPLÄTZE

Without a place to play every
child is handicapped.
Automatically.

If a child cannot break out of
the monotony of apartment house
ghettos, he will break in somewhere else out of boredom.

The fact is--juvenile vandalism
is the highest where children
have no place to play.

Help out today, so that it will
be better tomorrow.
For the children. For us all.

Support the work of the Kinder-
hilfswerks with an annual contri-
bution of 24 DM or a contribution
according to your evaluation.
Send to Post Office Bank Account
Number 440-809, BLZ 70010080.
Kinderhilfswerk, Langwieder,
Hauptstrasse 4,8000 Munich 60
Telephone 089/8142550 or 8141059.

Our goal--New playgrounds.

After explaining that it is virtually impossible to accurately measure the costs of vandalism, Britain's Central Policy Review Staff estimated the annual bill for damage to school buildings in 1979 at Ł15,000,000. If we compare this estimate of expenditure with the 600,000,000 dollar reckoning of annual loss in the United States, we find that American schools are expending more than four times as much per student as British schools.

We might conclude, by way of summary, that in Britain (a) the educators and students report little vandalism in their schools; but (b) the financial losses actually are considerable; and (c) these expenditures still are much less than those incurred in the United States.

Whether in England or America, the educational damage deriving from school vandalism is most difficult to assess. These costs are largely hidden but would include a very important waste of instructional time. Many teachers' hours are consumed in supervising, reprimanding, and disciplining the students; much of the administrators' time is devoted to various kinds of detective work for which they are most poorly prepared; while lots of innocent students' time is wasted on interrogations, false accusations, and "good citizenship" lectures.

School vandalism is psychologically debilitating, too. A gang of boys, for example, breaks into the school's commercial room and smashes up the typewriters. Parents hear about the break-in and are so incensed that they lose confidence in the school. Students, teachers, and administrators, greatly inconvenienced, become upset and angry at the turn of events. School custodians, who have been assigned the difficult task of keeping an already shoddy school building in repair, give it up as a hopeless job. Members of the board of trustees hear the bad news and feel their expenditure of time and money to help students has been largely wasted. The local newspaper features a page one story dealing with "Our Troubled Schoolrooms," and demands tougher security measures. And so feelings of exasperation, futility, disgust, alienation, and fear gradually come to pervade the school community. At this point it becomes impossible to put a price tag on the losses to education, but we should recognize that damage to property is of secondary importance and that the real victims are all the people in the victimized school.

EXPLANATIONS FOR THE DESTRUCTIVE ACTIONS

In the year 30 B.C. the poet Virgil authored the maxim, "Felix Potuit Rerum Cognoscere Causas." Although he was alluding to the study of husbandry, his observation that "Happy is he who has learned the causes of things" also holds true in the realm of school vandalism today. Those of us investigating the situation cannot claim to know the happiness of which Virgil spoke, since the causes of vandalism are still more theoretical than factual.

A starting point is the knowledge that adolescents commit most of our property destruction. Some authors refer to the years between 12 and 18 as a time of "flowering and fulfillment," while others call them "a calamity." If, in our efforts to account for school vandalism, we accept the latter description, then the turbulence so common during these psychologically stressful years can be explained in two ways.

One theory posits that puberty is a biological fact. This period of greatly accelerated maturation is heralded by what the English call "the endocrine commotion." Adolescents have varying degrees of difficulty adapting to their very rapid physiological developments, and often become physically awkward, unstable, and confused. The frustrations inherent in such bodily turmoil may be vented through destructive behavior.

A second viewpoint faults the socialization process. The child learns by imitation--first in the family, where parents, brothers, and sisters act as models; next in play groups, then in school, in the church, and from the mass media. He learns

one set of values in early childhood, but during
adolescence is exposed to a vast array of incon-
sistent values in the larger society. Intergener-
ational conflict and rapid cultural change introduce further complications, and the adolescent may
become emotionally unstable and anxious. He is
filled with exuberant, but yet unchanneled energy
during this span of time bridging childhood and
adulthood. He faces a multitude of adjustments
during this period and is not provided with a
well-defined role to play. He has not yet experienced the few available rites de passage, or cere-
monies indicative of adulthood, such as graduation,
marriage, or full-time employment, and yet he no
longer considers himself to be immature. As a
consequence, he asks to be treated as an adult but
reserves the right to act as a child.

Most people would agree that both the psychological and social problems noted above are con-
tributing causes of vandalism. Severino has gone
a step further in his recent doctoral dissertation.[3]
Arguing that vandalism is an outward manifestation
of inner trouble in the school, he offers specific
explanations for the large amounts of unwanted
destruction in American school buildings:

1. The decline of discipline in the home
   has led to "permissive parents" who
   encourage the irresponsible actions
   of their children.

2. Vandalism is an offshoot of campus
   violence. A "social revolution" is
   filtering down from the colleges and
   universities to our high schools and
   middle schools.

3. Students are protesting against the
   establishment. Today anyone over
   thirty years of age is old, and the
   teenagers are rebelling against them.

4. Vandalism is a reaction to poverty and
   racial discrimination. This is the

political and/or ideological explanation for the problem.

5. In suburbia, where taxes are high,
there is strong citizen hostility
to the costs of education. The
children hear their parents com-
plaining, adopt these belligerent
attitudes, and act on them by destroying school property.

In contrast to Severino's explanations, many
writers take the position that boredom is a primary
cause of vandalism. Erich Fromm, in his Theory of
Aggression, explained it this way: "Man is a pas-
sionate being in need of stimulation. He tolerates
boredom and monotony badly, and if he cannot take
a genuine interest in life, his boredom will force
him to seek it in the perverted way of destructiveness and violence." One may assume that property
destruction in the schools probably results not so
much from idleness and "nothing to do" boredom as
from a lack of challenges which provide incentive
and motivation in the students.

American television has repeatedly been cited
as a major cause for our increase in vandalism. In
the January, 1976, issue of The Phi Delta Kappan,
for example, a City University of New York professor
pointed to the United States Surgeon General's Investigation. That research effort was an exhaustive
three-year study set in motion by the Chairman of
the Senate Communications Subcommittee and dealt
with the impact of televised violence on children.
One conclusion drawn from that study and quoted in
the magazine noted above was:

"The more violence and aggression a youngster
sees on TV, regardless of his age, sex, or
social background, the more aggressive he
is likely to be in his own attitudes and
behavior. The effects are not limited to
youngsters who are in some way abnormal,
but rather were found in large numbers of
perfectly normal children."

British television, by contrast, provides a different sort of viewing. It features more educational, cultural, and public interest programs; it purveys many presentations with calm, low-key rather than aggressive and exciting qualities; it does not aggravate listeners with the meretricious appeals of all-too intermittent advertisers. Television viewing in England, therefore, cannot be considered a primary cause of the vandalism problem there.

In a survey of six secondary schools in West Norfolk, England, nearly half of 1,600 children 12 to 14 years of age confessed that they had willfully damaged property. When asked why, more than half of them said they committed these acts "to be big," nearly one-third of them gave "boredom" as the reason, and others said that they "lacked parental control," or were "too unintelligent to find a proper hobby."[4]

Poor grades in school have been cited as a cause for vandalism. The letter grades, or marks used in most of our school constitute rewards for the students. Unfortunately, however, not every student can be given A's, and many of those who get poor grades rapidly lose their zest for education. As a consequence, some of them become so discouraged and angry that they seek revenge; they act out their feeling that "We couldn't make our marks in school, so we'll make our marks on it."

Closely related is the idea that non-reading promotes aggressive reactions in children. In special schools which New York City has set up to take care of youngsters with behavior problems, test after test has shown a positive correlation between low reading ability and antisocial conduct. When a reading handicap begins to emerge the child does poorly in school. As he falls further and further behind, a spiralling process evolves in which the inability to read increases the child's disturbance and this disturbance creates a block against learning. His pride and ego suffer endless

wounds in the classroom, and having no normal outlets for these frustrations, the child reacts with
attempts to forcibly stop the educational machine
through vandalism.

Many other determining factors have been cited
for school vandalism in America. Inter alia these
include: the students' needs have not been met;
the community school concept has not been sufficiently developed; the school facilities have deteri-
orated, whether through accidental damage, misuse,
or ordinary wear and tear; and the teachers in today's "progressive" schools are too permissive.
The idea that today's adolescent difficulties are
being created by teachers has been rather persua-
sively discounted; to the contrary, what has been
overlooked in the hysteria over the vandalism dilemma
is that, for all its shortcomings, the school is the
most positive influence in the lives of many problem children.

School vandalism in Britain has been said to
be the result of: neglect in religious and moral
training; inadequate playground facilities; broken
homes; police ineptness and even corruption; unequal
distribution of wealth and income; students' low
test scores and marks; use of alcohol and drugs
(largely in older students); lack of adequate parental control and guidance; little provision for problem pupils (not providing what they call "sin bins"
and the like); inadequate personal and social conditioning; defective glandular functioning; youthful
maliciousness; failure to answer the fundamental
needs of students; poor home conditions; the doctrine
of easy money; lack of discipline in the schools;
changes in society--especially in attitudes toward
education and the teaching profession; lack of corporal punishment such as "caning" and "birching;"
failure to remove all obvious sources of temptation;
parents not being made to pay the cost of repairs;
failure to solve the problems of society; not providing a curriculum suitable for the students; and
lack of "close counseling by the pastoral system."
As in the United States, the list is endless.

School vandalism is sometimes interpreted as an environmental signal. In this sense it constitutes a form of phatic communication which is easy to see but most often difficult to decipher. A graffiti message in which a student proclaims that "John loves Mary" may be rather accurately interpreted. But what is the message being sent via our most common act of vandalism--tossing a rock through the school house window? And what is being communicated by the student who wads up wet paper and then throws the globs so that they stick to a restroom ceiling?

A final, rather inventive explanation of school vandalism is the sexual deprivation theory. This doctrine posits the advent of strange new bodily developments in adolescents which make for great sensitivity, inexplicable emotion, unwarranted embarrassment, and persistent acne--with a resulting perplexity which leads to aggressive behavior. Here acts of vandalism are seen as natural outbursts deriving from the unrequited strains of puberty. One can only wonder if the proponents of this idea would recommend that we retain a kind of Olympian calm while allowing free sexual activity to solve the problem.

In searching for causes some writers have tried to trace the etiology of school vandalism. This approach to the problem suggests that vandalism itself is a disease which afflicts the school. But such is not the case; vandalism, instead, should be interpreted as a symptom of sickness--a manifestation or sign of malaise in the victimized school. Physicians distinguish between different kinds of symptoms and their classification may prove to be helpful by way of analogy. They note that cardinal symptoms are those of greatest significance; that objective symptoms are those perceivable by others; that subjective symptoms are noticed only by the patient; and that signal symptoms are those which are indicative of attack.

What, then, are the cardinal symptoms of an unhealthy school situation? What are the objective symptoms which put the public on notice of inner problems? What are the signal symptoms which tell us to watch out for immediate danger? We are suggesting that school vandalism is definitely pathognomonic, that is, that school vandalism is distinctively characteristic of a diseased or pathological condition, and that it will flourish in an unhealthy educational environment.

Our problem, then, lies in what physicians would refer to as differential diagnosis--determining which of several diseases may be producing the vandalic symptoms. It appears that school vandalism, as a symptom, is multi-factorial, that it is produced by the joint action of several determinants, as suggested previously. At this point the problem becomes: What factors in the school situation should we stress in order to establish and maintain a healthy educational environment? What kinds of treatment will have the greatest overall curative effect on an ailing educational institution?

Specialists in health care differentiate between preventive and curative medicine. They ask, for example, whether it is preferable to invest in a water and sewage system for a city, or to pay later for treating infectious diseases. Reports from a recent magazine[5] are that today only two to two and a half percent of the health care monies in the United States are expended for preventive, as opposed to 97 1/2 to 98 percent for remedial or curative medicine. At the risk of overdrawing the medical illness/educational malaise analogy, one could ask a similar question about educational investments. Should the officials of a victimized school (a) invest 98 percent of designated moneys or programs designed to help students make proper adolescent adjustments, with the hope that they never consider resorting to vandalism? or (b) expend that allocation on attempts at imposing legal liability, i.e. for hiring lawyers to sue the vandals' parents? The former alternative is clearly preferable, but more expensive because it requires long-range, in-depth planning and execution.

ATTEMPTS TO STOP SCHOOL VANDALISM

Attempts to combat school vandalism have taken various forms in the United States. School administrators have initiated "get tough" policies and programs comprising corporal punishment, suspension, expulsion, heavy fines, and lawsuits. They have hired security forces to guard their buildings; they have elicited the help of local police, sheriffs' offices, and state police; they have set up elaborate systems of flood lighting and other after-dark illumination for the grounds; they have attempted to induce residents in the school area to report acts of vandalism. A number of schools have gone so far as to contract for the services of sentry dogs, usually large Doberman pinschers or German shepherds, and/or to hire police observors to hover over school playgrounds in a helicopter.

In the occasional case where the identity of the vandals is known, schools have tried making the offenders pay for the damage they caused. Some states, such as New Jersey, have passed laws making parents liable for the vandalic acts of their children, although ordinarily their liability may not exceed a certain prescribed legal limit.

Still other attempts to stop school vandalism have drawn on technological innovations. These efforts include installing audio detection and/or motion detection systems, vibration detection complexes, electronic and mechanical radar systems, surveillance cameras, photoelectronic beams, automatic telephone dialers, and ultrasonic communication devices. Several officials have purchased closed circuit television networks for their schools, while many have put in alarm systems, both fire and burglar. A few districts have acquired expensive intrusion and fire detection systems, while additional ones have erected heavy

chain-link fences and installed plastic glass in
their windows.

All of these attempts have been only partially
or temporarily successful in combating school vandalism. They have been largely ineffectual because
these measures strike only at the manifestation of
trouble, i.e., the vandalic act, rather than at its
underlying causes. While at times it may be necessary to resort to devices such as these, they should
be recognized for what they are--temporary, stop-gap
measures of limited utility.

Although the maximum security approach described
above has been recommended by school business officials and insurance companies for many years, research
has shown it to be quite costly as well as ineffective over long periods of time. Mechanisms such as
window alarms, office safes, and flood lights are
expensive. If employed, they should be kept as
simple as possible and used only when and where
necessary. Security personnel also command a high
price, and cost even more when given proper orientation and training. Their employment, in addition,
may be needed only at semester-end, when most break-
ins are known to occur (November and December, May
and June). We must conclude that limiting the use
of control devices is sensible in light of the expense involved, plus the knowledge that any positive effects are only short-term.

Another reason to minimize reliance on heavy
security measures is the likelihood that their use
may actually be counterproductive. Visible alarm
systems and security guards often worsen the already
"neopenal" architectural appearance so common in
our present-day school buildings. Some facilities,
for example, brandish bars over the classroom windows, or even worse, provide no windows at all.
Some schools are patrolled by uniformed guards,
while others are surrounded by prison-like fences
or walls which make them resemble fortresses.
Although designed to prevent property damage, such
heavy security measures may actually exacerbate an

already serious problem. Oftentimes, for example, they are interpreted by students as a message from the adult world delivered by the school system, saying "We can't trust you, so we're building walls and fences to stop the misbehavior we expect from you." This makes the innocent students (who usually constitute 95 percent of the student body) feel unfairly distrusted, trapped and resentful; and the student vandals inevitably rise to the challenge by learning how to outsmart the contrivances, or when this isn't possible, to devise more creative ways to damage school property.

In addition to the above considerations, school administrators should concern themselves with cost efficiency. It is important to compare the expense of a security measure with the amount of monetary loss which that measure is likely to prevent. Will employing a night watchman, for example, save his $10,000 salary in a year? How long will it take for a bigger alarm system with tamperproof locks and window grills to return its initial cost? What measures appear to be the best financial investments when projected over the next ten years?

Even the most carefully chosen security system, however, is not the answer to the school vandalism problem. What has failed in the past is not likely to succeed in the future, so rather than repeating those expensive errors of the past, it is time to attack the problem in a new way. The antivandalism efforts discussed thus far can be categorized as "deterrent" as opposed to "preventive" in nature. They are instituted to discourage property destruction through fear, while preventive efforts are based on provisions which anticipate and consequently avert the problem before it threatens. An old medical maxim advises us to "treat the cause, not the symptom," and such preventive approach will focus on the fundamental causes of school vandalism.

It is axiomatic that each set of circumstances must suggest its own remedies. Every school is

different in character and composition, with its
attributes being determined by the principal, by
students, by staff, by the community, and by the
physical environment. This is why a particular
antivandalism program may be highly successful
in one school and may not work at all in another,
and why even the most unlikely programs have had
favorable results in a few school situations. It
follows that each school should determine, to the
greatest extent possible, the underlying causes
of the vandalism from which it suffers, and then
apply preventive techniques which are appropriate
for its particular situation.

A very specific example of this approach is
provided by a school which has an unending problem with graffiti, and responds with the more
desirable preventive-type action of installing
palimpsests, or scribbling boards, which have
been found to provide a kind of deflection answer
for graffiti.

Proper preventive practices can make heavy
security measures unnecessary. They can resolve
many of our common educational deficiencies and
consequent debilitations, as well as the subsequent
environmental signals being sent out in the form
of vandalism. Among those approaches which provide promise of establishing a healthy educational
environment are the following:

1. It is generally accepted that the
principal, or head teacher, is the
most influential person in determining
school spirit. He or she sets the
tone and does much to boost or deflate
faculty/student morale. If the school
is to be a healthy one educationally,
he/she will need to institute an
equitable, firm, and consistent system of order, and make him/herself
highly visible to, and communicative
with students, teachers, and other
employees. One British teacher put
it this way: "A strong, capable

person must be made responsible for
the overall discipline of the school.
All members of staff must be given
an assurance that their sustained
efforts to maintain good standards
will be fully supported. The head
must also help and advise newly-
qualified teachers."

As part of being an educational leader, the
head person in a school should not only know what
constitutes a good physical learning environment,
but he/she needs to tell and to sell his or her
ideas to those persons having the power to make
it possible. This means that the administrator
will not be dallying with administrative trivia
such as counting lunch money, that he/she will not
get caught up in a daily stream of constant "emer-
gencies," and that he/she will not waste time
fostering punitive attitudes about property destruction.

It is important that the administrator spend
time promoting a humanistic, rather than an institutional zeitgeist for the school. One simple
example concerns the design of walkways, which
have so often been constructed only at 90 and 180
degree angles with respect to buildings. They
should be patterned to follow paths made by persons
coming into and leaving the structure, which means
that they can lie at any angle with relation to
the facility, or may take a semi-circular, para-
bolic, zig-zag, or other course. This type of
planning eliminates the need for "KEEP OFF THE
GRASS" signs. Every school's leader should use
his or her influence to promote a people-oriented
rather than a building-oriented school.

The head person should work to eliminate the
dull, boring, and standardized conditions which
encourage acts of vandalism in a school. This
means that he or she will oppose egg-crate school
building design (which makes all students file in
and out of classrooms), paved surfaces surrounded

by chain-link fences, uniform box-like rooms, fixed and rigid seating, colorless and textureless walls, and straight rows of desks, as well as lines of students in the cafeteria, playground, music room, or wherever.

In addition, both immediate and persistent action are important if the administrator is to keep the school well maintained. Any atmosphere of neglect or dereliction will evoke more and more destruction, as noted by one headmaster's observation that "One filthy word leads to ten others, if not immediately erased by scrubbing, painting, or sanding down." Persistence is an important factor in repairing damage, too; research has determined that when we replace quickly and often as needed, the vandals usually give up after three or four attempts.

2. Any program which involves students and makes them feel that it's their school will promote organizational good health. Even the very small percentage of students who are known to destroy property may, to quote an old adage, "be loath to bore holes in the bottom of a boat in which they are sailing." Furthermore, students who take pride in their school will put pressure on the would-be vandals to refrain from damaging school property. This is accomplished simply because students generally prefer to avoid the disapproval of their fellow classmates.

One major obstacle to the development of school spirit is the size of schools. Many of today's students are made to attend schools which are much too large. They have trouble finding the rooms where their classes meet, don't know the other students, haven't met any of the teachers, and perceive the administrator as some kind of far-removed potentate. They develop little feeling of belonging in such overcrowded environment and come to see themselves as mere anonymous entities.

This kind of school has proliferated in America because the cost per student is less than in smaller schools. A second justification is the claim that a large school provides a greater range of course offerings and extracurricular activities than several smaller schools. Today, however, it is becoming increasingly clear that so many educational problems derive from sheer size that the old "bigger is better" philosophy is largely apocryphal.

One proven way to encourage a healthy school is to provide students with many positive incentives. When students are encouraged by lots of rewards, prizes, and honors, they take part in a panoply of activities which eliminate free time and the resulting boredom and at the same time develop a feeling of involvement. A large share of our antivandalism efforts with students assume that we need only to inform them, to make them realize the costs and consequences of their actions. Unfortunately, most such programs of "education and enlightment" constitute only vague appeals for cooperation, and consequently fail. We should, instead, induce students to participate in projects which are designed to improve and to instill pride in the school.

Several California school districts, for example, have set up cash incentive programs. The administrators have said to the students, "Last year we spent $15,000 replacing broken window glasses and repairing other damage in this school. This fall we will put $15,000 into a special fund, and whatever amount of this is not expended for vandalism replacement, may be spent as you wish for class projects." Some parents have objected to this sort of program, asking "Why should we pay them not to vandalize?" Nevertheless, the approach has generally been successful. While this type of program does not focus on the fundamental causes of vandalism, it does provide a positive inducement to minimize vandalism and points the students' efforts in a worthwhile direction.

3. The advent of the community school was one of the most important trends in

British education during the 1960's and 1970's. This kind of school is planned to meet the community's needs, to encourage student use of facilities after, as well as during school hours, and to provide for adult educational and recreational activities as well. Its rooms are occupied, and consequently well-lighted and supervised after the customary eight to four o'clock day. Its institution and development have been found to promote a health educational environment.

Recognizing that much vandalism does occur after school hours and that it is most often committed in dark, unsupervised areas, some school districts have arranged for families to live in mobile homes adjacent to their school grounds. The people enlisted receive no special training, don't wear uniforms, and are not asked to patrol the area; but the mere presence of full-time residents on school grounds has, in many cases, discouraged property destruction.

A corollary to the community school concept concerns community involvement. If, in diagnosing a school situation, it can be determined that school vandalism is symptomatic of other, more serious social problems, then such action may be appropriate. Liverpool, England, for example, recently set up a low-key program involving parents, children, police, probation and social service workers, housing management, and community employees. These groups worked together to provide new, as well as to improve present recreational and social facilities. Area authorities reported that because the people had a hand in improving the community, they now care about it. They have noted, however, that many of the benefits of community development probably will not show for a number of years.

4. A final point is that the school
   facility itself can act as antidote
   for some of the ills of education.
   Although the notion would be difficult, if not impossible, to prove
   by research, common sense leads us
   to the conclusion that an attractive
   facility will discourage educational
   malaise. The ideal school building
   is a place where children want to be;
   it is so inviting and pleasant that
   it draws them to it in a magnetic
   way. This kind of school has classrooms which are aesthetically as well
   as functionally well-designed; the
   various spaces are planned in terms
   of the students' perspective and
   scale; it encourages free-flowing
   access in and out of the rooms; on
   the outside it has green grass, trees,
   and flowers which are growing; and
   inside it has walls which are covered
   with students' artwork and varied projects, showing that the emphasis is on
   learning rather than teaching.

If, as architects say, buildings communicate,
then an educational facility should say, "We value
young people." For decades our school buildings
provided horrible examples of a "monumental"
architectural style. They were designed to be
indestructible, to last a minimum of fifty to
seventy-five years, and to be antiseptically maintained. Today we have learned to think in terms
of flexibility, adaptability, expansibility, and
making our facilities home-like, rather than
institutional. Many research studies have con-
firmed the conclusion that carpeting in school
buildings, for example, not only saves money over
a period of years, but that it cuts down noise
level and makes the facility more comfortable,
thereby exerting a salutary influence on student
behavior.

Good architectural design can foster a healthy school environment. Zeisel, at the Graduate School of Design, Harvard University, has published a manual of practical suggestions for averting property destruction in new school buildings.[6] He recommends that builders avoid such architectural errors as hidden doorway niches, challenging accessible rooftops, unnecessary door hardware, reachable wall lettering, vulnerable playground windows, and misplaced pathways.

Newman, a British architect, has constructed a model for environments incorporating a hierarchy of private, semi-private, and public spaces.[7] He posits that (a) a lot of private or personal space is needed, and (b) public space is less prone to destructive acts if it is made to look like private space, or is related to adjoining buildings. Such ideas for inhibiting property destruction through physical expression could be put to use in school facility design. There is no question but that children need personal space, space to hide in, space to retreat to, and that most present-day schools provide a highly standardized environment with little such space.

The importance of the architectural issue should not be under-estimated. It has been said that architecture shapes the feelings of people more than any other art form because people cannot withdraw from a building as easily as they can retreat from a painting or piece of sculpture. Winston Churchill once observed that "We shape our buildings and then they shape us." It follows that architects, working with educators and others, have a special responsibility to design school facilities which will encourage creative learning rather than destructiveness.

SUMMARY

Vandalism in American public schools has become a major financial consideration. Many of its costs are hidden, only a fraction of the damage is reported, and still fewer of the offenders are ever caught. While financial losses from school vandalism are large, the educational losses incurred are recognized as being of even greater importance.

The typical school vandal is presented in profile. A description of the circumstances in which he operates, a delineation of the victimized school, and a compilation of words used to categorize and describe vandalism are provided for administrators concerned with the locus of the problem.

Many causal factors are cited for school vandalism. Prominent among these are rapid biological maturing, faulty socialization, student boredom, American television, and reading difficulties. Vandalism is observed to be a symptom of malaise in the victim school, and noted as often being multi-factorial in origin.

Heavy control devices have been only partially or temporarily successful in obviating school vandalism. This is so because maximum security measures treat the situation only symptomatically, rather than getting at the roots, or proximate causes of the problem.

Although many observors feel that school vandalism will continue to constitute a major administrative concern during the coming years, such need not be the case. Positive preventive approaches which will resolve many of our common educational deficiencies and consequent debilitations, as well as the subsequent environmental signals which are being sent out in the form of vandalism, are suggested.

NOTES

1. Birch Bayh, Nature, Extent, and Cost of School Violence and Vandalism, Congressional Subcommittee to Investigate Juvenile Delinquency, Washington, D.C.: Report of the United States Committee on the Judiciary, 1976.

2. Vandalism, A Note by the Central Policy Review Staff, Cabinet Office, Her Majesty's Stationery Office, London, April, 1979.

3. Michael Severino, "School Vandalism: Legal Implications," Ed.D. Dissertation, University of Denver, 1971.

4. Daily Telegraph, London, England, September 9, 1979, p. 8.

5. Daedalus, The Journal of American Academy of Arts and Sciences, "Doing Better and Feeling Worse: Health in the United States," Winter, 1977, p. 65.

6. John Zeisel, Stopping School Property Damage, American Association of School Administrators, 1801 North Moore Street, Arlington, Virginia, 1976.

7. Oscar Newman, Defensible Space: People and Design in the Violent City, Architectural Press, London, England, 1972.

CHAPTER VII

FACILITY MAINTENANCE

AND REMODELING

Maintenance was mentioned briefly in a previous chapter where the cleaning program of the school's custodians was discussed, and should be distinguished from "housekeeping." Housekeeping or plant operation does not call for repair or replacement; maintenance does, although in popular usage, maintenance may also refer to cleaning. The custodian for most schools will be the person who will be alert to observe maintenance problems and will take care of them or inform the administrator so that a maintenance specialist can be secured for a particular job.

Preventive maintenance is essential for a well managed school. It is not wise to wait for something to break down or wear out before giving it attention. The following statements focus on the major facility maintenance activities that most administrators will encounter when managing their facilities.

SCHOOL PAINTING

A painting maintenance schedule should be prepared to indicate need for painting and planning painting time for school classrooms, corridors, and exteriors. A custodian can be very faithful in cleaning walls and ceilings, but if the paint is old and worn, his work will be practically worthless because it will not look any better or cleaner.

There are many plans to follow in designing a good maintenance schedule. These plans must face the constraints within the maintenance budget. In most instances the administrator looks to the central office specialist or the professional painter for estimates on the job. In large districts there may be maintenance men whose only job is painting according to the district-wide schedule. This has its advantages where contracting with professional painters is prohibitive in cost. It may even be necessary to use custodial personnel. Obviously, the administrator's concerns are eased where painting is a central office and not a building administrator's decision.

Weekends, Christmas, Easter, and summer vacation periods provide the time for painting schedules. It is best not to try to do the work all at one time; many school districts do all their painting during the summer. If custodians are used to do the work during the summer, problems may be encountered in fulfilling other major cleaning and maintenance chores. Spreading the painting workload over a year will allow the time of personnel, both custodians and professional, to be used most efficiently. Planning and charting the painting program will aid in developing an efficient approach to reducing the usual school painting problems.

The administrator or his custodial staff probably know nothing (or very little) about indoor or outdoor painting. The administrator should turn to specialists inside the district or in industry for advice. Appropriate color and color combinations cost no more than those that do little to enhance the aesthetics or building decor. There is no longer any valid excuse for having a dull looking building. Imagination and good taste can provide the right color combinations for both interior and exterior. Some paint distributors provide the services of a color consultant. How some have solved their school painting problems was described by L.F. Williams in "How to Cover Your School Painting Headaches."[1]

ROOF MAINTENANCE

Roof maintenance usually waits until an emergency strikes such as a roof leak somewhere in the building. Maintenance results in keeping the roof in good repair and avoiding such experiences or at least keeping them to the bare minimum.

The administrator may include an inspection of the roof during the annual inventory of building needs. If competent roofing people are available, they may be employed to join the inspection. The roofing specialist has the experience and training to detect impending roof problems that escape the eye of the layman. Also, he should be able to give some fairly close estimates on the cost of yearly roof maintenance or the costs for putting the roof in good repair. The cost of a good roof might possibly be far less than maintenance cost for a short period of years. Most roof coverings are not constructed to last the lifetime of the building. Beware of those who pass through your area claiming that roof troubles can be eliminated once and for all with some highly touted roof materials. The addition each year of costly roof patching materials can easily cost more than the construction of a new roof and drainage system designed especially for your climate and building.

A number of preventive cleaning and maintenance tasks should be completed on a school roof. Most roofs have some kind of a bond that guarantees the condition of the roof for five, ten, fifteen, or twenty years. It is necessary to check with the people who provide the roof bond concerning your responsibilities versus their responsibilities in regard to cleaning and maintenance of the roof. Much like the part and labor guarantee on a car, if you do something to jeopardize your guarantee, then the roofing company may devoid themselves of responsibility.

Roger Riedel, roofing superintendent for the state of Wisconsin, provides a quality service list

for roof maintenance that is acceptable for all
bonded roofs. The services are:

1. Keep the roof free of standing water
    at all times. Clean drains at least
    twice a year--spring and fall. Clean
    all the strainers, outlets, and gutters
    and carry the debris away...do not leave
    it on the roof. Standing water is harm-
    ful both winter and summer to all kinds
    of roofs, especially one which has built-
    in deficiencies.

2. Remove collections of leaves from corners
    of parapets on the roof. This policy
    will prevent obstruction of the outlets
    and also permit the roofing to dry quicker.

3. Check that all counterflashing is secure.
    Caulk and paint as necessary to keep it
    from deteriorating. Such metalwork is
    not included in the bond agreement.

4. Place and maintain approved platforms
    (such as waterproof plywood) at points
    where traffic is heavy, such as at hatches
    and doors leading to the roof, and at
    machines which require frequent attention.

5. Check immediately after storms to promptly
    discover any damage to base flashings,
    counterflashings, skylights, expansion
    joints, etc., which could result in leak-
    age. Call in an approved roofer for
    prompt repairs if professional service
    is delayed.

6. Observe the behavior of the roofing as
    it ages, whether the base flashing is
    pulling away or slipping, or if promi-
    nent wrinkles are developing or cracks
    appearing. These signs foretell trouble.
    Make temporary repairs with plastic ce-
    ment, but consult an expert in roofing
    for analysis and correction.

7. If metal edging such as gravel stops have been used, check for the development of cracks in the joints between lengths of metal as the roof ages. The action of metal edging as it expands and contracts will crack the surface plies of the roofing, eventually permitting leakage. Since the bonding company is not responsible for metal upon roofing, it is a problem of maintenance.

So much for bonded roofs. For other roofs not under bond, all the above items apply plus the following:

8. Where joints in the surface ply of base flashing appear to be open, apply a troweling of roof cement, reinforcing membrane (asbestos, felt, treated jute, or glass fabric) and finish with a generous weather coat of cement to completely conceal the reinforcement.

9. Small breaks or blisters on smooth-surfaced roofs (ungraveled) or built-up roofs are easy to repair when bone dry, using asphalt roofing cement and the previously mentioned reinforcements. Aluminum roof paint of good quality can be expected to shield the roofing from deteriorative effects for five years.[2]

A member of the custodial staff should be charged with the responsibility of checking, inspecting, and maintaining your roof following the above or similar guidelines. Many roof problems can be eliminated with a good preventive maintenance program.

WINDOWS

Many problems arise in maintaining windows in an older building. Wooden window frames need frequent inspection to determine the effect of weather exposure which can cause rotting of the frames. Occasionally, the wooden frames will loosen from masonry walls and cause air leaks and jamming of the window frame and sill. A careful check for caulking deficiencies plus frequent painting will provide most of the maintenance requirements. From time to time putty will dry out or leak air or moisture around window panes. Old putty should be removed and replaced with new putty and painted. Painting protects the putty from drying out and normally keeps it in good condition for a number of years.

Cracked or broken panes of windows become a safety hazard for students. Reglazing of windows should take place as soon as possible. Custodians can quickly learn to replace window panes. Replacement glass can be pre-cut and stored for use. Glass can be cut for size in the custodians' work area or purchased from local hardware or glass stores. A putty knife, putty, a pair of pliers, and glazier's points will fulfill the equipment requirements for reglazing. Recently, broken or cracked school window panes have been replaced with plastic panes. The possibility of breakage is reduced. It would probably be a good idea to experiment with plastic window panes to see if this should be a part of your maintenance program.

Many window maintenance people say that window frames (wood and steel) require painting every two years, three, four, five, etc. The best approach is to check at least once a year and paint when necessary. If they show signs of blistering, fading, or peeling, then it is time to paint. Detecting painting needs early will check serious window maintenance problems.

DOORS

Exterior doors for most school facilities are subject to heavy usage. A problem often found in older buildings is that the hardware is not of duty construction and cannot take the jolts and slams

-206-

of continuous usage. The solution is simple--
specify heavy hardware replacements to reduce
door problems and maintenance.

Wired glass should be used in all exterior
doors when glass is desired. Wire glass provides
greater safety for students because this glass
normally will not fall out or in, thereby pro-
tecting the student from jagged edges and flying
glass. Using wired glass as replacement glass on
doors should help to eliminate some safety and
maintenance problems.

Another routine maintenance job is to check
fire exit panic bar door devices. This takes a
minimum of time to check and it should be done
daily by the custodian. One slow opening or
jammed door can cause a panic situation when
used during a peak traffic time. A routine check
for faulty operation of door holders and door
closers will prevent damage to the door and to
wall areas near the doors. If the door holder is
faulty, the door will probably swing open too far
and damage the wall it opens to or it could damage
the hinge, causing the door to close improperly.
The simple procedure of checking door handles,
lock, and latch areas to see if screws are tight
and using graphite on open working parts such as
the bolt head will also help eliminate many future
door operation problems.

SCHOOL LANDSCAPE

Shirley Cooper, a man who contributed so much
to encourage the development of well planned school
plants, felt deeply about the aesthetic value of
the school. He was certain that among many things
the facility should be beautiful to the eyes of the
students and the community. He said:

> "With a look toward the future, the school
> building reflects the ambitions, the hopes,
> the aspirations, and the dreams of a people
> that is striving to move forward and upward

to a way of life that is better, fuller,
richer, and more rewarding than that
which it now knows. At its best in form
and appearance--as it stands majestically
on the highest hilltop in the village, or
nestles quietly and unobtrusively on the
bank of the small stream in the valley,
or affcrds a pleasing contrast to the
dull, monotonous tones of a tenement
district in a congested metropolitan
area--it is an expression of the aesthetic values of the people and their sense
of what is pleasing and beautiful."3

The development and maintenance of school landscape can provide an outside environment that sets
the pattern for quality education. Many people
judge what they see outside the school facility as
the true picture of the school. There does appear
to be a relationship between care and maintenance
of grounds and general attitudes of staff and student about the importance and value of school and
education.

An administrator can do something about the
outside school environment. School landscaping,
unfortunately, is given less attention by the
administrator than most other areas of responsibility. A landscaping plan should be developed.
This planning should be accomplished in cooperation with a landscape designer. Too many school
sites have been landscaped almost entirely on the
whim and fancy of people or groups who have donated
plants, shrubs, trees, and flowers to be planted in
the absence of overall design. A system must be
constructed for developing and maintaining school
landscapes. The major components of landscaping
are turfing, shade trees, shrubs, plants, flowers,
paved areas, paths, walks, pools, benches, tables,
and other seating areas. With imagination and
planning, the administrator, the designer, and
others can lay out a pleasing landscaping program.

For immediate landscape improvement, an administrator can prescribe a routine maintenance plan to
cut and trim grass, shrubs, and trees so that they
look cared for. It is surprising how the raking of
leaves and debris will improve an area. Just the
spading and turning over of dirt in planting areas
changes the whole aspect of the outside landscape.

What are some of the important considerations
to take into account concerning landscaping and
maintenance?

1. In most instances an automatic sprinkling
   system should be utilized. Ordinarily
   the custodian's time is limited and the
   assignment of additional responsibilities
   to carry hoses, move sprinklers, check
   faucets, etc., will reduce his efficiency
   in other cleaning and maintenance areas.
   An automatic sprinkling system provides
   an easy way to water on schedule instead
   of the hit and miss approach with the hose
   or when the custodian can get to it.

2. Concrete strips should be placed under
   fence areas where the area is covered
   with grass. The strips will allow the
   mowing equipment to come close enough
   to the fence areas to cut the grass
   and will eliminate the tedious and
   time-consuming job of trimming grass
   areas around fences. The time saved
   in having to trim the grass will pay
   for the construction of the concrete
   strips.

3. Types of turf, shrubs, trees, and plants
   to be used in the landscaping plan must
   be selected in light of their economical
   care and minimum water requirements.
   Each area throughout the United States
   has particular weather and soil conditions that lend themselves to certain
   grasses and foliage. If the care and

maintenance operation for particular plantings is extensive, then a bad choice has been made and this should be changed.

4. Types and methods of fertilization must be experimented with and then established. One cannot depend upon media advertising to make decisions on what to use. A competent gardener, soil conservation people, or others should be engaged to help make the best decision concerning the soil conditioning program. Many soil areas around schools have been damaged because of the misuse of soil conditioning materials.

5. The careful selection and use of equipment is a prime source of labor economy. When designing a landscape plan, determine the kind of equipment necessary to maintain the area. Equipment maintenance and purchase is usually a knotty problem for most schools. Small schools with small landscape areas and schools with a low landscape maintenance budget may rent equipment as needed. This will allow the work to be done without the cost of purchase or cost of maintaining and storing equipment.

6. The use of a variety of seating arrangements in your landscape design aids in developing a feeling that it belongs to students and is for their use. Landscape areas that feature large signs reading "Keep Off Grass" provide a feeling that the area is to be looked at rather than used for educational purposes or recreation.

Elementary school grounds can be
enhanced by providing realistic and
colorful playground equipment. Manufacturers of playground equipment
can simulate moon rockets, satellites,
space slides, radar towers, flying
saucers, a submarine, lighthouse,
fantasy fish slides, a crow's nest,
prairie schooners, corrals, cactus
climbers, and tepees, to name only
a few, to stimulate the imagination
and interest of elementary children
at play. All may be constructed out
of plastic, steel, and concrete materials for safety and ease of maintenance. These colorful, interesting,
and safe products provide an appealing
situation for young people and create
a feeling that school is an inviting
place to be. Perhaps budget restrictions will limit the number of these
play objects that can be purchased
at one time. However, with a master
landscaping plan, some could be added
each year.

For the elementary and junior high
schools, bicycle racks should be provided. The racks should be placed in
an area that will allow bike traffic
with a minimum of congestion. Also,
racks should be placed so that they
can be easily observed by staff to
minimize tampering or possible thiev-
ery. Many companies will supply a
choice of a variety of bicycle racks.
Custodians and/or maintenance specialists in the district could make the
racks.

For elementary, junior high, and senior
high it is suggested that benches be
provided throughout the campus area.
They should be colorful and at the same

time blend in with the total landscape design. A variety of benches
are available in steel, wood, and
concrete. All should be selected
on the basis of student utility.
The addition of seating area in the
landscape design adds to the overall
beauty and aesthetic quality.

7. It is quite easy to fall into the trap
    of landscaping those areas of the
    school that are most likely to be seen
    by the public. Don't neglect the back
    areas of the school or those plots be-
    tween classrooms and adjacent to walk-
    ways. The total acreage should be
    developed and maintained with the
    thought of economy of time and labor
    as a major design factor.

8. One of the most important considerations
    for landscaping design is the assignment
    of manpower to care for the area. A
    carefully structured schedule should
    be prepared for each custodian. He
    should know exactly what outside
    ground areas are his responsibility.
    There should be directions for watering,
    mowing, cutting, trimming, and general
    cleanup of leaves, papers, and other
    materials. The schedule should take
    into consideration the time of the
    year. In many sections of our country
    winter weather will inhibit outside
    work and reduce the time to be spent
    in care and maintenance during the
    cold season.

    To develop a specific number of min-
    utes for each outside task requires
    a great deal of experimentation. The
    task of establishing a formula for man-
    power outside maintenance is not easy.
    One superintendent developed a man-

power schedule based on an allotment
formula for an elementary school.[4]
Such a formula represents only one
of the many approaches to manpower
utilization. Each administrator
should develop his or her own schedule of landscape maintenance because
of the peculiarities of land use,
vegetation, and water requirement.
No one formula will suffice for all
schools or a majority of schools
across the country.

THE VALUE OF MAINTENANCE

An effective method of measuring the vision,
efficiency, and the values of a school's administration might be the observation of its comprehensive maintenance program. The leadership in such
a program must be supplied by the administrator.
There must be policy, procedure, and the development of a system approach to see that costly public
facilities represented in the school are being
maintained and conserved to the best interests of
the educational program, the students, and the
general public. A school building is an educational tool and it should be maintained to give
its most effective service in the learning process.
If its well kept and well repaired appearance helps
to create an ideal learning environment for students
and conveys to them a feeling that schools are a
most important factor in their lives, then any
amount of effort and concentration of quality
plant maintenance will be of inestimable value.

SCHOOL FACILITY REMODELING

Remodeling is gaining in popularity to accommodate the many educational program innovations
that are now being implemented throughout the
country which demand some physical changes in the
older facility. Many school districts do not have
the tax base to provide the funds for the required
new facilities. They turn instead to remodeling

their old facilities or purchasing used commercial or industrial plants and remodeling them for school purposes.

Because of the press for additional facilities in the larger urban areas, some school districts have experimented with the purchase of industrial and commercial structures that are being sold because of a move by the occupants to suburban shopping marts or industrial parks. Many of these structures can be gutted and remodeled to meet the educational needs of students. There are a number of examples of this approach to remodeling across the country and we can anticipate that it will increase.

The Philadelphia Board of Education has considered the purchase and conversion of commercial and industrial structures for use as teaching facilities. A case study titled "The Loft Building as a School House: A Study for the School District of Philadelphia," by Murphy Levy Wurman,[5] made possible by a grant from Educational Facilities Laboratories, Inc., aims specifically at investigating the possibilities and limitations of conversion. The case study findings revealed that conversion has great potentialities which more than offset the limiting factors.

Remodeling for Teacher Preparation Space

Perhaps the major responsibility of the school administrator is to maintain a high quality of instruction within his school. One of his considerations should be to determine what he can do for the staff that will enhance its teaching effectiveness.

Today there is a great push to develop a three-pronged approach to organizing staff and students. Reference here is to (1) large group instruction where large numbers of students learn from expertly prepared presentations of subject matter; (2) small group instruction where 12-15 students learn through discussion with teachers and other students; and

(3) independent study where students learn largely by themselves. This approach to learning or personnel organization requires the teacher to do more things in the act of preparation. Although the teacher is asked to do many things, what kind of space is provided for the teacher's preparation?

Teachers need an appropriate place to perform their professional work. They are expected to continue developing their knowledge about teaching. We expect the teacher to introduce new ideas in a variety of ways. There are records to keep. Evaluation of students' work is of prime importance. However, little consideration is given to improving the space in which the teacher accomplishes the above.

A booklet prepared by Raymond Schneider[6] focuses on teacher space where more than one person will work at one time. Space is required to plan and prepare lessons, develop instructional materials, and to confer with others (staff, parents, students, and administration). Space for teachers, according to Schneider, should be provided at many places throughout the school plant. How can anything be done about teacher space if it was not included in the school when it was constructed? Remodeling is a prime alternative.

First one must determine what kind of teacher spaces are needed. Then one should take a look at present storage areas, library area, administration office space, and classroom space to see if some of that area could be rearranged to provide more teacher production space. Many kinds of space dividers can be used to close off areas. In some instances file cabinets can be used as space enclosures. Furniture and equipment can be arranged to section off areas. Imagination and a will to develop adequte teacher work space usually leads to a solution of the remodeling problem.

Facing the Remodeling Problem
=============================

Many times remodeling will cost a great deal less than providing new additions or a new facility. However, this is not always true. Some older facilities will require great structural changes as well as fire and safety code demands when remodeling is anticipated. Costs can be so great under these circumstances as to make remodeling impractical.

Many structural considerations are involved in remodeling that have little or nothing to do with the kind of student program that will take place in the remodeled area. What can be done to assess the remodeling problem? The A.A.S.A. provides a remodeling evaluative procedure for an existing building. Their checklist is:

1. Site

    a. Is the site large enough? Are better alternate sites available?

    b. Are visible site elements such as sidewalks, fences, and parking areas in adequate condition?

    c. Do existing utility services provide adequate capacity to meet program demands?

    d. Does the site drain properly?

    e. Are there subsurface soil problems which may cause structural difficulties on the site?

2. Structure

    a. Are there any signs of deterioration or failure of footings, foundations, or piers?

b. What is the structural framing system (steel, wood, or reinforced concrete)? Do such clues as moisture penetration of walls or roofs, sagging floors, sticking windows and doors, or cracking of walls or ceilings suggest the possibility of structural deterioration?

c. What is the general condition of visible elements of the building such as windows, floors, wall and ceiling surfaces, the roof, flashings, sprouts, lockers, and hardware?

3. Mechanical and Electrical Facilities

Are such elements as heating, ventilation, and cooling systems; plumbing fixtures and piping; and electrical systems such as lighting, outlets, conduit, public address, and program in adequate condition? Are they accessible so they can be modified in a remodeling program without extremely high cost?

4. Code Requirements

Any evaluation of an existing building must include a highly detailed analysis of its ability to meet the requirements of applicable building codes. This analysis will answer such questions as:

a. Are exit facilities such as corridors and stairways adequate to allow rapid and safe egress?

b. Does the building provide fire resistive ratings required by the code?

c. Do floors and roofs have ability to carry loads established by code requirements?

d. Are adequate light levels provided? Adequate numbers of plumbing fixtures? Acceptable numbers of air changes?

5. Cost

Needless to say, the cost factor is of prime importance and may well be the deciding factor in the final analysis.[7]

The question to be answered: Is it worth the cost of remodeling? The administrator should suggest that an evaluation of the building be made. An architect or a consulting engineer should be given the task. They are trained for this kind of work and it should be a fairly routine assignment to determine the structural condition of the facility and the costs involved to bring it up to a desired level of repair. To make decisions and statements about your structure without the advice from architects or consulting engineers is fool-hardy. Most administrators are not trained to make these evaluations and should not think of accepting that responsibility.

What kind of information would be found in a written report of a consulting engineer after evaluating a facility? His major purpose normally is to list the structural and fire and safety code deficiencies. The following is a hypothetical sample of a school building evaluation report by a consulting engineer.

School A
Structural and Building Code Deficiency List

This building is classified in accordance with Uniform Building Code, 1972 edition, as Type III N. Deficiencies are as follows:

1. Table No. 5D prohibits more than one (1) story in type III N construction with Group C occupancy. Two (2) story requires type III one hour. An approved sprinkler system may be instituted for the one hour requirement.

2. Section 802b requires type I construction up to and including the first floor. This requirement cannot be readily complied with except by abandoning and sealing off the basement which would necessitate relocation of heating plant and storage space.

3. Toilet facilities do not comply with requirements of Section 805 as to number of fixtures or Section 1711 as to finish of floors and walls.

4. Draft stops should be provided in the attic as required by Section 3205.

5. Corridor doors from classrooms should swing out as required by Section 3318d and should be solid core doors with closers as required by Section 3304.

6. Stair landings should have splayed corners and north stair should be cut off from basement with one hour separation at first floor.

7. Illuminated exit signs should be provided as required by Section 3312.

8. Electrical system should be revised to conform to current code requirements. Work required principally consists of replacing some sections of exposed wiring with metal raceway.

9. North and south walls of gymnasium exceed height to thickness ratios given in table No. 24-I, and should have some intermediate support.

-219-

10. Masonry work is generally in good condition, but should be pointed up particularly along parapet walls.

Basically, the structure appears to be sound and structurally adequate with minor exceptions as noted in the attached list. Some deficiencies as noted exist in provision for fire and panic consisting principally of a non-conforming type of construction for the number of stories and occupancy. The electrical system is in part non-conforming and some replacement should be made.

The following alterations and repairs are recommended:

1. Installation of an approved sprinkler system.

2. Seal off basement and provide separate heating plant.

3. Refinish toilet rooms and add required fixtures.

4. Provide draft stops in attic space to subdivide into 2500 s.f. max. areas.

5. Replace all corridor-classroom doors and close transoms.

6. Revise electrical system as required and add illuminated exit signs.

7. Repair all masonry and provide intermediate bracing for gymnasium end walls.

Estimated Cost of Repairs

Item	Description	Cost
1.	Fire Sprinkler System	$17,500
2.	Heating Plant and Seal Basement	20,000

3.	Toilet Rooms	5,000
4.	Draft Stops	1,000
5.	Replace Doors	2,000
6.	Revise Electrical Systems	2,500
7.	Point and Brace Masonry	2,000
	TOTAL	$50,000

Signed: John Smith
Consulting Engineer

The $50,000 estimated by the engineer reflects only the costs of making the facility structurally sound and meeting fire and safety code requirements. The estimated cost of facility changes to meet the demands of the school program are yet to come. These costs can only be determined when the architect knows what functions and activities will be held in the spaces to be modeled.

Educational specifications must also be developed for the remodeling of a facility. The process is the same as that specified previously for the development of educational specifications for a new building. It is imperative to describe for the architect the desired function of the proposed area to be remodeled. To do less would seriously limit the possibilities for a quality remodeling design.

SUMMARY

School facility maintenance by and large over the years has been neglected in most school districts. It appears to be the one thing in the budget that can be easily passed over. What happens, however, is that somewhere down the line the costs for major maintenance repairs occur and these costs wipe out many proposed instructional activities. Administrators have the responsibility to pay some attention to the preventive maintenance aspects of their facility. Their attention with a systematic approach will enhance the operation of their schools. The items of maintenance that require scrutiny on a regular basis are outside and inside surface painting, roof areas, windows, doors, school landscape, and general facility appearance. The value of preventive maintenance relates highly to reduced maintenance costs. In addition, there are other supportive reasons for a good maintenance program, such as:

1. A school facility is an educational tool and must be maintained to provide the most effective service for supporting the learning process.

2. If the school's well-kept and well-repaired appearance helps to convey to students that the school is important in their lives, then this is valuable.

3. The school facility is seen almost daily by many people who support the funding of the school's operation. Most people will have more positive feelings on supporting a school's endeavor when it appears that someone cares for maintaining and watching out for their investment.

Major school facility remodeling activities are now occurring throughout many school districts. The primary reasons for remodeling activities today are due to fiscal problems that exist country-wide to support constructing new facilities and by remodeling many school facilities can function with new program requirements. Some large city school districts are purchasing industrial and other commercial structures that are being sold because the company is moving to the suburbs or elsewhere. These structures are usually gutted to the building shell and then remodeled to meet the educational needs of the student program. Conversion of these structures has proven very satisfactory for a number of districts.

If the remodeling effort is more than just changing a door, or one wall, then a structural engineer or architect should be asked to survey and inspect the area to be remodeled. The costs may outweigh the benefits of remodeling if the structural, safety, and fire code requirements dictate bringing many things like wiring, sanitary facilities, structural, and other deficiencies up to date. The structural engineer or architect should provide estimated costs of remodeling based upon the building code requirements and educational requirements. The educational facility requirements should be provided by the administrator and should include educational specifications describing the activities and related spaces you desire.

NOTES

1.   L.F. Williams, "How to Cover Your School Painting Headaches," School Management (July, 1966): pp. 148-149.

2.   Roger G. Riedel, "Highest of Problems--the Roof," The American School Board Journal (April, 1966): p. 33. Used by permission.

3.   Dr. Shirley Cooper, Schools for America (Washington, D.C.: American Association of School Administrators, Commission on School Buildings, 1967): p. ix. Used by permission.

4.   Charles Knight, "Manpower: Important Factor In: Grounds Care Know-How," The American School Board Journal (June, 1967): pp. 38-40. Used by permission.

5.   Murphy Levy Wurman, The Loft Building as a School House: A Study for the School District of Philadelphia (New York: Educational Facilities Laboratory, Inc., 1968): p. 39. Used by permission.

6.   Raymond C. Schneider, Space for Teachers (Stanford, California: School of Education, Stanford University, Western Regional Center Educational Facilities Laboratories, Inc., 1967). Used by permission.

7.   Cooper, Schools for America, p. 127.

CHAPTER VIII

EDUCATIONAL ISSUES

AND THE FACILITY

A number of emerging issues concerning education today will have influence on the planning of future facilities. This last chapter reflects some thinking on a few of the emerging education issues that should concern the administrator and the school district when undertaking facility planning activities.

ENVIRONMENTAL EDUCATION

The status of environmental education today is in limbo. Many educators are talking about it but doing very little. The few programs that exist contain many inadequacies. The Minnesota Environmental Science Center,[1] national leaders in environmental education, have stated the following inadequacies in environmental education:

1. There exists no coherent philosophy of environmental education.

2. There is a lack of teacher interest and background training.

3. No comprehensive school program in environmental education exists at present.

4. There is a paucity of curricular software relating to environmental education.

5. Collegiate training programs are inadequate.

6. There is no effective leadership or coordination in the area of environmental education which would provide for quality training programs and information systems.

Even though great inadequacies exist concerning environmental education, it is important that educators take hold and provide the physical spaces for learning environmental concepts. Students must get outside the school's walls to observe the many happenings within the environment. With not too great an expense, but with a great deal of imagination and creativity, the outside land area of the school could serve as excellent study areas.

For the most part, little thought is given by educational facility planners or architects to developing school sites to serve at least partially as environmental learning areas. Usually the architect strips all or most of the natural vegetation from the land and destroys water areas. The land area around the school can be so arranged that students can utilize it to learn basic concepts about air, water, land and their influence on man.

The Minnesota Science Center, in Minneapolis, has developed a number of concepts concerning the establishment of mini-environmental systems on the school ground area. Some of the ideas include the following:

1. A number of exciting alternatives exist for the educational development of enclosed spaces and alcoves formed by building configurations. These spaces usually are enclosed on all sides with a controlled access or formed by three walls, opening directly onto the school grounds. They typically receive little traffic by students and are relatively

non-functional in the educational
program. If consideration is given
to the types of plants introduced
into these spaces, a school can have
at its disposal a continuing variety
of flowers, berries, and fruit used
by insects and birds. Students can
study the plant materials and the
organisms using them.

2. During the school year, students
often plant seeds in milk cartons
or small flower pots for observation.
Generally, the plants are allowed to
flourish for a few weeks. They are
then discarded <u>before</u> the exciting
facets of growth and maturation are
fully explored. The problem is usually a lack of space needed by young
plants after they are beyond the
seeding stage. An alternative suggestion is to transplant the seedlings
from the classroom to planters located
outdoors where rainfall and light will
most nearly approach growing conditions.
Planters can be made from discarded
railroad ties, posts, telephone piles,
or pulpsticks dipped in penta or creo-
sote. Each classroom could have access
to an experimental plot. Students
should be responsible for its care
and maintenance. Plant materials can
be solicited from interested parents,
garden clubs, local service organizations, or landscape nurseries.

3. Animal and bird feeding stations can
be established. The variety of living
things that visit a school site will
be substantially increased by these
facilities. Surprisingly, animals
and birds become accustomed to being
observed from a distance. Sometimes
small animals can be attracted by

-227-

placing food such as acorns, walnuts,
pine cones, and sunflower seeds in a
specific observation land space on
the campus. Not all sites are conducive to this kind of activity,
especially those located within the
center of the large urban city.

4. Other facilities can be established
    such as poly-ponds, experimental
    gardens, decomposition study plots
    and outdoor mapping areas.[2]

The above are but a few of the many things
that can be undertaken to plan for an efficient
use of the school's outdoor space to enhance the
school's environmental education program. The
program for each school will vary; however, there
is no reason why outdoor facilities cannot be provided if the administrator and his/her staff plan
with the architect to incorporate the outdoors
area into the total environmental learning process.

SPACE FOR EDUCATING HANDICAPPED STUDENTS

A recent survey found that less than half of
the school districts in the United States now
provide specialized programs for handicapped
children. Those districts that do provide programs usually provide a bare minimum approach.
One of the few districts that provides an effective
long range continuing effort toward educating the
handicapped is Peoria, Illinois. There, students
are provided with a program that is heavily focused
on career education starting in the early grades.
Materials, activities, spaces are provided to
insure success for the handicapped student.
Peoria's approach to the handicapped student is
the exception and not the rule.

Some thought has been given by educators of
the handicapped that many handicapped students are
not learning well in segregated spaces. We find
that some alternatives have been developed to

provide special support services to the handicapped child placed in the regular classroom. Where fully adequate supporting services have been provided, it appears there have been positive learning experiences for the handicapped student, the normal student, and the teacher.

At present, we need about 300,000 more teachers of the handicapped to fill the needs of handicapped students. It appears that it will be ten to fifteen years before training institutions of higher learning will start to fill that gap. Therefore, it is essential that planning be accomplished to provide program and facility space in a variety of ways so that the handicapped student can succeed.

Planning facility space for handicapped students requires that the program activities be closely analyzed and then designed to accommodate the functions. Teachers of the handicapped student are good sources of information to provide those suggestions that could facilitate the design of the building to be used by the handicapped student. They would suggest that:

1. Special consideration should be given to providing elevator services if it is a multi-story facility.

2. Ramps for wheelchairs or students with walking problems must be designed.

3. Door widths should be wide enough to allow passage of wheelchairs and other transportation aids or devices.

4. Doors should be designed to be opened very easily. See-through doors are necessary so that handicapped students can see beyond the door and anticipate problems that might arise when someone else is about to open the door.

5. Wider corridors are needed for wheelchairs and greater walking space.

6. Safety features must be designed for use of the bathroom, playground, and multi-use areas so that students with a variety of handicaps can participate in a logical sequential manner.

Designing facilities that can be used by the handicapped student is a problem because very few educators have taken the time to discuss and decide what are the essential activities, materials, and devices that are required within spaces to adequately service the handicapped student. The architect normally will follow your instructions in this area because it will, for the most part, be his first exposure to this kind of a design problem.

SPACES FOR CAREER EDUCATION

When Sidney Marland was U.S. Commissioner of Education, he urged that great emphasis be placed on a career education program for all who can benefit. National funds have been provided to develop a school based career education model, an industry based career education model, and a community based career education model. The authors believe that the two latter models, when fully developed, will be utilized to support the school based career education model to carry out the total program. With great focus on career education now and in the future, we must consider how this will influence the school facility.

There will be greater use of the facilities of industry and business on a cooperative basis with the schools. For most secondary schools, there will be greater student exploration activities of many occupations and their related skills rather than learning specific skills. Planning should focus on providing a greater variety of equipment rather than row upon row of machine lathes, welding machines, drill presses, etc. Many secondary schools will still have the dual purpose of providing career education for the secondary student, adult education, and post-secondary programs.

This poses the problem of utilizing a facility both day and night for many different purposes. This trend will continue and will become common in a few years because of the great demand on the tax dollar. School facilities will have to serve more people, a wider variety of people for longer periods of time during the year, as well as all hours of the day.

Some special space requirements must be considered for the secondary school facility that additionally must provide for adult education and post-secondary programs. The trend, now and for the future, is providing flexibility of space in construction over providing special fixed spaces for particular career education programs. Today, we see a rising surge toward training in many different medical occupations, office occupations, and specific technical skills related to data processing and electronic devices designed to serve mankind. However, a great deal of information indicates there will be many rapid changes in technology that will demand training in a wide array of skills that at present do not exist. Therefore, secondary vocational facilities should be planned with the great possible flexibility to accommodate many different kinds of training programs that will evolve from the demands of our future labor force.

The word "flexibility" is easy to use but hard to define when describing flexibility of facility space. Schools will have to utilize a variety of learning groups. Some part of the training program will provide exposure to learning in large group situations, other skills and concepts can be better learned in small group situations, and certain elements of the training can be best accomplished by placing the student in an individual study or learning situation. The instructional groupings cited above call for a variety of space sizes and functional capabilities.

A variety of spaces combined with effective scheduling can also provide flexibility in the use of the facility. Some of these spaces might be quite specialized: office machine laboratory, data processing unit, drafting work areas, or a cosmetology training center. Other spaces should provide for varying degrees of multi-use capability.

Another mode of flexibility is the ability to change space immediately with a minimum of effort. Such changes are apt to be necessary during the day and generally take the form of temporarily reducing or expanding spaces in order to separate or bring together groups or activities. This flexibility can be accomplished primarily by movable walls in the framework of continuous floors and ceilings. To maximize the inherent versatility of such a facility, care must be taken to place utility lines so that they will in no way diminish adaptability. Movable furniture, portable equipment, and space dividers that are easily moved by teachers and students will enhance the possibilities of flexibility.

Long-range changeability is also an important component of facility flexibility. The design of the building should permit rearrangement of interior partitions in order to facilitate change in programs and the resulting redistribution of students, teachers, and equipment for a period of time. Just the ability to move interior partitions will not provide maximum flexibility. Special consideration should also be given to the ability to relocate electric outlets, switches, lighting fixtures, supply and return air diffusers, ductwork, thermostats, etc. This leads to flexibility in changing control of lighting, heating, and traffic zones within the facility. These change possibilities should be planned so that regular school maintenance personnel can do the work in a short time with minimal help from outside labor.

The final consideration of facility flexibility is planning for the expansion of the building so

that increases in enrollment and special spaces
may be accommodated by an orderly expansion. A
minimum of interruption, cost, and demolitions
should be planned for in the expansion design.
One major problem of expansion in the past has
been the increase of heating requirements and
extension of the general mechanical system.
Using a component of a utilized heating-venti-
lating-air-conditioning system as a solution to
the expansion of a mechanical system shows great
possibilities.

The career education oriented school of the
future should have a large outer shell with inside
space that can be easily divided, subdivided, or
enlarged to accommodate the program needs of its
students throughout the year. Equipment, for the
most part, must be movable, not fixed to the floor
or wall, so that it will not inhibit variety of
space uses required for day and night students.

THE EDUCATIONAL PARK

The architectural firm of Caudill, Rowlett,
and Scott of Houston, Texas, developed a document
titled, "Educational Park--A Case Study Based on
Planning and Design for Anniston, Alabama." Donald
B. Wines, AIA, a school building specialist for
Caudill, Rowlett, and Scott, had this to say about
the history of Educational Park in that document:

> "The Educational Park dates back to the
> turn of the century when Preston Search
> proposed a 200-acre site to house the
> entire school system of Los Angeles.
> He felt that a healthy farm environment,
> away from smoking chimneys and congested
> urban conditions, could lead to uncon-
> scious instruction.
>
> He emphasized that his school park would
> be more than a traditional educational
> institution—it would be a cultural center,
> a library, vacation farm school, and a

meeting place for people of all ages.
Economically, there would be a savings
due to shared facilities and optimum
scheduling.

Preston Search was obviously well ahead
of his time. Since then the basic themes
he established for the park, i.e, a pastoral setting, the school as a community
center, the park as a means of educational
innovation, and the park as an economy
measure, have recurred in one way or another,
but rarely have educational parks actually
been built and never have they approached
their full potential.

In the 1930's, an educational park was
built in Detroit, Michigan, primarily for
economic advantage. In 1946, in Glencoe,
Illinois, an educational park was built
combining community and educational facilities for adults and children. In 1958, an
educational park was built in New Orleans,
Louisiana, again for economic reasons."[3]

There are other educational parks operating
today such as the one in Broward County, Florida,
known as the Nova Educational Park. The cities of
Chicago and Pittsburgh have spent many months and
years planning for educational park enterprises
within their cities.

The basic concept of the educational park
complex provides an educational program for pre-
kindergarten to post-high school education. The
educational park can provide a great wealth of
staff, materials, equipment, and special facilities
in close proximity to a variety of students and
great quantity of students. This complex should
provide a greater continuity of program for students because of the possibilities of closer
interaction of staff and students and use of
facilities at all levels. More efficient use of
land could probably be attained under the park

concept. The large urban areas are the most likely locations for utilizing the educational park concept. Planning for such a large facility is time consuming and should involve many people to coordinate the total effort.

Some educators totally refute the idea of developing such a large and grand facility primarily because they feel it would be impossible to administer. They also feel that it places the students in a maze of buildings that will overwhelm them and deter their essential learning activities. Proponents of the educational park feel that the student has a greater chance than ever to succeed because he has everything readily available in the way of staff, material, equipment, special spaces, and equality of education with his peers.

Donald Leu listed advantages and disadvantages in a presentation made at the 1967 annual meeting of the Council of Educational Facility Planners:

> "Some of the advantages I see associated with the 'Educational Park' are:
>
> 1. By bringing together children of a wide range of economic, social, religious, and cultural backgrounds, they tend to overcome the narrowing influences of severely stratified neighborhoods.
>
> 2. They reduce inequalities of facilities, staff, and program so characteristic of neighborhood schools.
>
> 3. They provide a more widely common set of experiences that lead to better communication with the total community.
>
> 4. They facilitate the grouping and re-grouping of children on the basis of desired educational objectives.

5. They would offer advantages of services and facilities commonly attributed to size.

6. In large cities, they would offer the opportunity for largely self-contained decentralization.

7. They provide unique possibilities for flexible organization.

8. Greater curriculum individualization and pupil assignment flexibility would be possible.

9. By removing children from the immediate neighborhood, they could extend the opportunity for the development of mutual respect among different groups and cultures.

10. They would increase the availability of certain specialists who now spend considerable time traveling between schools.

11. There would be real possibilities for economy in many supporting services.

12. There would be opportunity to facilitate the operation of released time programs by religious bodies.

13. They provide the opportunity to free ourselves of burdensome tradition, to break from the existing mold and to re-examine existing principles and practices.

Having touched on some of the potential advantages of the 'Eduational Park,' let us consider what appear to be disadvantages. Let us briefly examine the other side of the coin.

1. The school with its related after-school services would be lost to the neighborhood.

2. Teachers, having been removed from the neighborhood, would have less opportunity to know and understand the child's environment and family circumstances.

3. They would cause fears of alienation of children from home and neighborhood.

4. Transportation problems for parents and children would result in terms of cost, time, and over-utilization of streets and transit facilities.

5. School accessibility to parents would be reduced.

6. They may cause little children to mingle too early, travel long distances, and cope with large numbers in huge, complex organizations.

7. They would run all the risks of bureaucracy, rules, and procedures.

8. They would provide a strong temptation to reduce variety, plan too efficiently, and build too rigidly.

9. The large costs of such complexes would be more difficult to "sell" than would be those of much smaller school units.

10. They would cause the abandonment of many schools that are still structurally sound and paid for.

11. The 'Educational Park' constitutes a single, huge facility that would move massively and uniformly toward obsolescence.[4]

Educational parks can solve a number of educational problems for inner city youth. The light-
hearted should not undertake the planning process.
Like any endeavor that is complex, provisions should
be made to provide for as great a planning time factor as possible and to involve the best talent, student, staff, and community alike. The Educational
Park or a similar concept will be one answer for
certain large city educational problems for many
years to come. The concept influences a facility
design quite different from the usual school facility
structure.

IMPLICATIONS OF NEW TECHNOLOGY

Each day we can read about new educational
technology or technology that can be readily adapted
to educational activities. Transition to the use of
technology is increasing in the classroom and other
school learning environments. Utilization of technology may be enhanced or inhibited by its spatial
demands. Technology that influences instruction and
that will affect administration roles should be
studied for cost effectiveness and then used if the
payoff is substantial. A word of caution is that
there are many pieces of equipment but not all will
do the job. Educational functions and activities
must first be decided upon and listed. Then,
technological devices should be tested to see how
well they assist in providing the required educational functions and activities.

When selecting equipment, one should certainly
pay attention to cost. However, another very important fact to consider is how easy it is for staff
and students to learn to use the equipment, and
whether other factors (such as lack of mobility,
and maintenance) will make utilization difficult.
Many language laboratories were purchased over the
past decade by many school districts. Many today
are used sparsely because of the difficulty in
managing and operating them, or because the lab
does not produce what was intended. Technology is
here and we must use it, but evaluate its utility

and be sure that it is worth the output of teacher and student time and effort before buying.

Many types of technology with many functions are ready for installation. Tomorrow there will be many more. The following provides some insight and review on some devices that are available now.

Communication Technology

It is essential for a school facility to have the ability to provide a variety of communication sources. The Bell Telephone System and associated companies suggest many educational uses of components of the telephone system. Some of these communication processes are the Tele-Lecture, Tele-writing, Code-a-phone, and Rapidial-Automatic Dialing Set.

a. Tele-Lecture provides the opportunity for a classroom of students to communicate with specialists in many fields of endeavor over special telephone loud speaker equipment. Two, three, four, or more classes in other schools could be a part of the same communication by providing a conference call situation. The resource person may speak over any ordinary telephone, over any distance, without need for supplementary equipment. He may speak at the same time to one audience or several, even thousands of miles apart. Communication is two-way, so listeners may question the speaker. This does not have to be confined to one speaker but a panel or several speakers across the country could participate. A number of schools around the country have taken advantage of the Tele-Lecture concept and have communicated with people at high level positions in government and industry. Use of Tele-Lecture has been made to provide in-service training for school staff.

The cost for installing the telephone jack for the telephone loud speaker is nominal and the rental on the phone speaker system is nominal also.

Toll rates for phone use are minimal, and when divided into the number of students who could participate in the Tele-Lecture, the cost per student would be low but yet very beneficial. The cost of bringing the top person in the country, on any subject, into the classroom or school by telephone for half an hour could prob- ably be done for twenty-five to thirty dollars. Student exposure to great talent can be made very cheaply. Most people, specialists in a particular field, would not mind sitting at their office desk to discuss a particular subject. This is an edu- cational equipment program opportunity that few schools are now taking advantage of.

b. <u>Telewriting</u>, operating over Bell System Data Phone data communications service or private line, makes it possible for a distant speaker to supplement his Tele-Lecture presentation with hand- written notes or drawings projected onto a screen before the listening and viewing group. Thus the presenter can be clearly followed as he works out a model, a formula, an architectural design con- cept, or diagrams which aid in explaining his con- cepts. The notes and diagrams are enlarged on the viewing screen for the student audience. In some ways, this media provides better graphic presen- tation possibilities than if the presenter appeared in person. Line and equipment charges are higher than the Tele-Lecture, but are reasonable for selected presenters whose ideas and concepts can expose students within the school to new learning experiences.

c. <u>Code-a-phone</u> answers your questions any time you wish. It can reply with any recorded message up to three minutes long, in the administrator's voice or that of other school personnel. It oper- ates automatically whether you are out or just prefer not to be interrupted. You may tell callers where you are, when you will be back, or give any particular information you wish. The message can be changed easily and quickly. Your callers always get an answer. The Code-a-phone can never miss a call. A special feature continuously assures the caller that the recorder is operating. You may monitor incoming calls with built-in speaker as they are being recorded and break in to answer personally any emergency calls. The Code-a-phone stops automatically when caller's message ends. You can play back messages immediately upon your return or at your convenience. An indicator tells how much has been recorded in your absence. Messages may be played over and over to insure accuracy in case of questions as all are recorded on tape. A foot control and headset permit easy transcribing by the secretary. The phone may also be used in the regular way.

Utilizing the Code-a-phone can free the secretary to continue on with scheduled work without many interruptions. She can handle the phone messages at her convenience. It provides the administrator with a good checklist on those phone calls that should receive high priority and attention. The Code-a-phone can and should be utilized to enhance the efficiency of the time and effort of the administrator and his/her staff during the school day and night. The possibilities for practical use are varied and numerous.

d. Rapidial-Automatic Dialing Set eliminates the need to look up numbers. A magnetic tape and index store the telephone numbers required by your general activities. It speedily completes local, long distance, and intercom calls, with no re-starting when calling through a dial PBX. The magnetic tape stores up to 290 fourteen-digit numbers. Numbers may easily be recorded and changed. It is easy to use. More calls can be completed faster during a day. Time and effort saving features let secretaries, staff, and adminis-trator make many more calls daily or spend less time making calls than by manual dialing. There is no capital investment. With an automatic dialing system, it is necessary only to turn a selection knob to the desired listing on the index, lift the telephone receiver, and push start bar after dialtone is heard.

Tele-Lecture, Telewriting, Code-a-phone and Rapidial could be used efficiently in a school facility. Telephone companies across the country have many other systems and pieces of equipment that could be successfully utilized in the school setting. It is necessary that facility planning include the exploration of the best possible communications network for the money available for this component of the facility. In the years ahead many breakthroughs will be made in the communications industry that will be beneficial to include in the school facility for administration, instructional, and recreational uses.

Computer Use

The computer can be utilized in many ways to enhance the school program. At present, there is some use of the computer for recordkeeping concerning school enrollment, pupil achievement, attendance, scheduling, and other specific data about students and staff. The computer is also used to provide computer assisted instruction. The computerized instructional program is the planned sequence of presentation of curriculum material. A computer system is able to process stored information by reacting to a specific instruction for each procedural step. The student is led through the curriculum in sequential steps with the computer systems dispersing information, then asking questions about it, going ahead, explaining, or repeating, depending on the answers given by the student using the computer instructional program. A computer-assisted instructional program is only as good as the input of the data. The cost of computer assisted instruction is many times more than the cost of traditional instruction.

An Educational Facilities Laboratory Report of April, 1970, discussed the computer assisted instruction system thoroughly. Some of the excerpts from that document are as follows:

1. The cost of development of high quality effective computer programs is difficult to predict. It has been estimated that for tuition of medium complexity, an average of 100 hours of author time is involved in development of one hour of student console time. But for complex tutorial programs, development time might be eight to ten times more.

2. Software companies are usually able to write and tailor their programs to the hardware that is most suitable and, therefore, able to exploit any special attributes that one piece of hardware might have. The industry is presently more experimental than commercial with federally assisted funding.

3. When CAI comes into use, it will probably not be on a schoolwide basis, i.e., one or two specific and confined areas of a school may be set up for CAI, probably in conjunction with only one or two disciplines such as math or the language skills. The terminators could either be connected to a remote computer shared by several school systems and managed by a software service company of a university center, or they might be connected to a local school computer which might be also used for administration purposes, especially in a large school system.

4. There are many crucial decisions which must be made at the design stage by the appropriate authorities regarding the possible use of computers and CAI, even if this use is not for several years. If installation costs were not continually rising, it would still be a great deal more expensive to remodel schools to make provisions

to accommodate future installations.
However, provision of unlimited flexibility for possible future changes is
unrealistic, and some parameters will
need to be set.

5. The strategy of the design team must
be that the building systems will
easily accommodate a remodeling program when electronic teaching aids
arrive in any quantity.[5]

The use of the computer in school systems for
administration purposes to make management decisions and store data is now underway in many districts across the country. Computer use for instruction is almost nil because of costs, minimum
programs, and lack of technicians and teachers to
operate the system. The age of the computer for
educational purposes is here and planning for its
future use must be a part of the master facility
planning schedule.

Multi-Media Information Retrieval

Some public schools today have a dial/select,
student operated system of retrieving audio-visual
instructional aids from a central library or media
source. The dial/select system allows participants
to select appropriate learning and teaching aids
for their immediate use. A dial/select system
center will have a variety of equipment and software. The extent of the equipment and software
depends upon the program development of the
particular school district and the amount of
dollars directed to the endeavor. Normally one
should find videotape recorders, audiotape decks,
commercial and closed circuit TV channels, tele-
casting of 16mm film, 35mm slides, and 35mm
filmstrips.

Students should have available dial/select
carrels in sufficient number so that they can make
efficient use of the equipment. There are many

possibilities for program activities for students at all levels. The initial costs are high for equipment and software, but if planning is focused on good student learning activities, the payoff can be appreciable.

THE YEAR-ROUND SCHOOL OPERATION

The year-long school operation is now being looked at very closely by many school districts across the nation. Actually, some types of year-round operation took place as early as 1904 in Indiana, and 1912 in Newark, New Jersey. Almost every year some school district somewhere in this country has been experimenting with the year-round school.

There is a great press today from many groups such as taxpayers associations, political sub-divisions other than school districts, women's public service associations, and others to start using the public school facility for longer periods of time during the day, night, and year. The primary reason for this push is to realize a greater return on the facility investment. Also, demands on the tax dollar from all sectors is heavy and avenues must be opened that will stretch that tax dollar to provide the best services for the populace.

There are a variety of year-round operation designs. Some would utilize a quarter system, others overlapping quarters, such as found in the 45-15 plan, another would include two semesters and the summer. Regardless of the plan, the intent would be to utilize the facilities on a year-round basis with a fairly well balanced population of students in the facilities at all times.

What are the implications for planning a facility that will be used on a year-round basis? Certainly better attention must be given to the quality of materials in regard to the ease of maintenance and care. No longer will the custodial staff have the whole summer to clean, polish, wax, paint, sweep, vacuum, etc. There will have to be a cleaning and maintenance schedule that will focus almost entirely on early morning, all night, and weekend custodial activities. It appears that the year-round school will probably require a complete air conditioning system to accommodate the summer heat prevalent in most, but not all, geographic areas of the United States. In addition to quality low maintenance materials and air conditioning, there will be additional requirements for the facility to use carpet for practically all floor surfaces because of ease of maintenance. A reduction of window space to a minimum will be required so that window cleaning and care will be a small part of the custodian's workload. Greater attention will have to be given to providing larger inside spaces for physical education because inclement weather prevalent during the particular time of the year some students will attend school. Somewhat larger administration spaces will be required, especially in those areas where student records are kept, but this will be a minimal additional facility expense.

There is no doubt that the school could provide for an additional load of students if open for the entire year. It is logical to believe that this would reduce the amount of capital investment for facilities over a period of several years. Again, with quality facility planning, there is no reason why a school facility could not be used all year by students and the community. There is no justifiable argument either in terms of cost or efficiency to say that the facility could not stand year-round use. Banks, factories, universities, all types of industry, municipal, state, and federal facilities are utilized the entire year. Schools will be forced to do the same in the years ahead. Facility planning must provide a design that will accommodate this kind of extended facility use.

THE FUTURE AND SCHOOL FACILITIES

Most educators today are having a difficult time keeping up with today's educational problems and their solutions and have little or no focus on the future. Today, more than ever before in the lifetime of our country, educational practices within the pre-elementary, elementary, secondary, and post-secondary schools will have a great bearing on the course our country will pursue. Evaluating where we are and when we must change in education must be high on our priority list of immediate activities. The educational program constructed for the future will have significant bearing on the number, design, and placement of school spaces.

There is good indication that within the next ten to fifteen years all kinds of teaching and learning devices, both hardware and software, will be available for purchase, lease, and use. It is well within reason that learning experiences linked to the total education program will take place within the dwelling unit of the student, and in a number of different areas within the community such as the store front school, the industry-based learning space, and the regular school location. Large study areas similar to present public libraries will be established within each large city and will be used by all members of the community. A great deal of individualized study activities will be available at all levels and can be utilized day and night.

At least one-half of the time of the student at all levels except the primary grades will be spent in educational learning experiences out of the immediate school setting. Older students will be exposed to a variety of business and industry on-site occupations and related skills. Younger children will explore the business and industrial world around them and its influence on their lives. Heavy focus will be made on the environmental control factors that are in use and how they can be improved. This will require a great deal of exposure to looking at, touching, seeing facilities, and talking to people involved in providing water, power, transportation, and sanitary conditions within a community. Again, a part of this time not spent in immediate school facilities will be spent in the use of the public information depositories that will be developed with all kinds of information retrieval devices. It will be too costly then as it is now for each school to have this capability.

At first it would appear that if students are going to spend less time in the facility than has been true during the past, that fewer facilities will have to be constructed over the next ten to fifteen year period. This is reinforced by the notion calling for year-round utilization of facilities and the fact that the birthrate may continue to decrease from record levels. These factors suggest a declining public school enrollment in the future.

However, another factor looms before us: what will happen to enrollments in parochial and other private schools in the years ahead? This thought deserves some consideration. Enrollments in parochial schools will probably decline to a point where these schools will service only about 10-15 percent of their present clientele. In other words, 90 percent of those in parochial schools today will be in public schools tomorrow. The private schools may remain about the same as today. This probable enrollment shift to the public school is an important factor which must be analyzed and included in all school district master facility plans for the next ten to fifteen years (if there are parochial schools operating presently within the district or nearby).

A trend today of demands for an expanding program for adult education will mean that, in less than ten years, adults will be the largest group of people served by the public school system. The adult education program will serve more population than will be served at the elementary and secondary levels. This has great implications for the school facility design. Public school facilities will certainly have to continue to serve adult education, but even in a much better way than now. Planning for this is imperative.

Many writers in the past have expressed what the future held for us. From Confusius to Malthus, we find underestimates of change. Orwell, a few years ago, appeared to be "way out"; today, and especially tomorrow, we will find that change has come quicker and in a wider range. Today a number of writers are predicting what the future holds for education. As a summary for this short discussion on the future and facilities, we will use some comments by S.J. Knezevich. He stated:

> "The configuration and operational characteristics of learning centers, presently called attendance units or schools, will be notably different in 1985. The many reasons behind this change were discussed previously; the movement toward "womb-to-tomb" educational programs; the new technology which will open new vistas and generate new and exciting learning strategies; and the reconceptualization of the teacher's role within the centers. Related to these is the fact that the computer will be as common in the home in 1985 as a television set is today. Computer utilities will supply computer services to homes in a pattern not unlike that for electric, telephone, gas, and other utilities. A more complete electronic link between home and schools will open a number of new options for the design of learning centers that were not practical prior to 1985.
>
> It is projected that new and exotic materials and new breakthroughs in special forms (e.g. geodesic domes) created by more sophisticated architectural engineering will find their way in

school facility design and construction throughout this and subsequent decades. In addition, the design of instructional, study, and special service spaces in schools of the 1980's will show the impact of the great variety of electronic teaching-learning gear such as computers, lasers, and holograms. In short, the internal arrangement of spaces and external appearance of the school facility in the 1980's will depart even more radically from present configurations than 1970 designs differ from those produced in 1920. The size and complexity of increasingly more specialized learning facilities will encourage the development of independent clusters of educational units rather than placing all under one roof.

Learning is a social process as well as an intellectual endeavor. Were it not for the social dimension, there may be less need for bringing the learner to a learning center of some type. The alternative future which suggests that the school plant, or learning center, where students are concentrated will disappear by 1985 or even 2000 is rejected for a variety of reasons. The alternative to clustering learners in a school facility is directing learning experiences into the home, or in some cases, to the place of work or another social institution. This option need not preclude the existence of a formal learning center with specialized equipment which cannot be placed, because of economics or optimum utilization, in each home. Not all learners will have to come to a school plant, but most will. The home may be an extension of but will not be a replacement for the formal school centers. Many futurists speak of the diminishing influence of the family upon groups and society. The living or interaction problems in many homes, particularly in what are called ghetto areas, suggest as well that it may not be the ideal locus for all learning activities. The Job Corps, as a residential educational institution in the 1960's, was designed purposely to remove some types of learners from a home environment that did more to bring on failure than promote success."[6]

There is one basic philosophical change that will occur in educational programs and that is the heavy emphasis on education for all rather than the college or university bound student. Today that trend is seen as the focus on career education from grades K-14. Tomorrow it will be called something else, but the basic fact is that we can no longer support the development of facilities and operation of an educational program that aids a few and neglects the rest.

SUMMARY

Emerging educational issues today will influence planning for future facilities. The issues of environmental education, educating handicapped students, career education, the educational park, use of new technology, the year-round school, and reduced enrollments in parochial schools should have great impact on future facility design.

The school in the late 1980's and 1990's will be serving more people with a wider range of grade levels and ages, and for longer times during the day, night, and year than it is now. In fact, the adult school population will be greater than the combined elementary and secondary school enrollments. In addition to utilizing the school facilities, we will find at least one-half of the student's time spent at teaching and learning stations outside the main school facility. Some will be heavily involved in learning skills at business and industrial facilities, others will be observing a variety of occupations at a number of different business and industrial establishments. Students will be involved heavily with environmental education and will use the parks, the fields, the health departments, sanitation departments, water departments, industry, and many others as much-used bases of learning operations. We will also see large multi-media centers constructed in central areas of cities and communities to accommodate the educational needs of all people within the community. They will contain a vast array of technology hardware and software. Individual schools will not be able to meet the high costs of excellent technology for learning; therefore, the large community all-purpose media center will emerge with many different financial sources of support.

Implications for the facility of the future will dictate that tremendous effort on designing for flexibility will have to occur--flexibility to change spaces immediately with a minimum effort--flexibility to expand the facility with a minimum of cost and demolition. The use of a unitized heating-ventilating air conditioning system as a solution to the expansion of the mechanical system shows great possibilities.

The school of today, for tomorrow's use, should have a large outer shell with inside space that can be easily divided, subdivided, or enlarged to accommodate the program needs of the school population throughout the year. Equipment and furniture, for the most part, must be movable, stored easily when required, not fixed to the floor or wall surfaces, so that it can provide a wide array of teaching and learning spaces for a variety of programs that will be used by students day and night throughout the entire year.

NOTES

1. Edward B. Kaiser, Environmental Planning Recommendations (Minneapolis, Minn.: Environmental Science Center, 1969). Used by permission.

2. Planning a School Environment (Minneapolis, Minn.: Environmental Science Center, 1970). Used by permission.

3. Caudill, Rowlett, and Scott, Educational Park--A Case Study Based on Planning and Design for Anniston, Alabama (Houston, Texas: 1968). Used by permission.

4. Donald J. Leu, "Educational Parks--The National Scene," in Council of Educational Facility Planners, Educational Facilities in Urban Settings (Proceedings of the 44th Annual Meeting, 1967).

5. Educational Facilities Laboratory, Instructional Hardware/A Guide to Architectural Requirements (New York: April, 1970). Used by permission.

6. S.J. Knezevich, Educational Futurism, 1985: Challenges for Schools and Their Administrators (Berkeley, Calif.: McCutchan Publishing Co., 1971). Used by permission.

REVIEW QUESTIONS

1. List and describe the five components which make up what, today, we call "school facilties" and in former years were referred to as "the school plant."

2. Who should be the members of "the planning team" for a new school facility? What should the role of each of these members be?

3. Point out several reasons why the selection of a site is important in school building planning.

4. What does research say concerning the effects of visual environment on the successes or failures in learning?

5. What does research say concerning the effects of thermal environment on the successes or failures in learning?

6. What does research say concerning the effects of acoustical environment on the successes or failures in learning?

7. Make a list of the contributions of carpeting toward making for a desirable acoustical environment.

8. What guidelines would you use in selecting colors for the interior spaces of a school?

9. Relate the legend of Procrustes with school building planning. From your experience give

an example of Procrustean planning and then
compare the school building which would result
when we use functional, artistic educational
planning.

10. What items would you include in a "Guide for
Preparing Educational Specifications"?

11. What are some of the more important educational
needs of students enrolled in the middle school?

12. List the innovative trends that have occurred
in recent years in the following areas:

    A. Curriculum
    B. Administrative organization
    C. Physical facilities

13. A. Define the following terms:

      (1) Adaptability
      (2) Flexibility
      (3) Expansibility

    B. Give an example of each of these educa-
tional facility dimensions.

14. What are the three statements suggested as
possible parts of a basic philosophy for an
elementary school program? What do you feel
should be included in such statement of basic
philosophy?

15. Outline a good in-service program for staff
utilization of a new educational facility.

16. What are some of the possible ways to buy furniture and equipment for new facilities, remodeled
areas, or new additions to a school building?

17. Give several guidelines which would help in
selecting furniture and equipment for an educational facility.

18. Why is it important to provide adequate and useful storage for equipment and supplies within a new facility? Give some suggestions for solving the storage problems which may arise.

19. Distinguish between OVERCROWDING and ADEQUACY of a school building. How can these concepts be measured?

20. Discuss the determination of student capacity for a secondary school.

21. What do you consider to be the most important points in Ed Feldman's Maintenance Program Quiz?

22. List the qualifications for which you would look when employing a school custodian.

23. Outline the basic steps in:

    A. Care of carpeted floors
    B. Care of washroom areas

24. Give suggestions for establishing and maintaining effective teacher-student-custodian relationships in a school.

25. How does the legend of Sisyphus relate with the school vandalism problem? Has vandalism been a problem in schools with which you have been familiar?

26. What measures would you, as a school administrator, initiate in your school to limit vandalism?

27. How can school facility design help to prevent vandalism? Give examples.

28. Outline an adequate program for school safety at one of these levels:

A. Elementary
B. Junior high school
C. Senior high school

29. Give suggestions for a policy statement dealing with the after-hour use of a school facility.

30. Make a list of ideas for preventive maintenance in the following areas:

A. School painting
B. Roof maintenance
C. Windows
D. Doors

31. What are some of the important considerations to take into account concerning school landscaping and its maintenance?

32. What factors should be considered in assessing the remodeling problem?

33. Discuss the effects of the following emerging educational issues on planning future facilities:

A. Environmental education
B. Educating handicapped students
C. Career education

34. What impact will the following issues likely have on future facility design?

A. Use of new technology
B. The year-round school